How To
Take Your Family Camping

Ken Gallacher

BK Publishing
P.O. Box 1211
Riverton, UT 84065

First printing February 1996
10 9 8 7 6 5 4 3 2 1

ISBN 0-9651054-0-7

Library of Congress Catalog Card Number 96-96060

Illustrations and design by Douglass Cole of Cairo Design Group
Front cover and inside back cover photographs by Rip Black
Design and typesetting by L. Jane Clayson

ATTENTION: The author, publisher, and all other persons directly or indirectly involved with *How to Take Your Family Camping* assume no liability for any misinterpretation of information contained herein nor for any accidents, injury, or losses by individuals or groups using this publication.

In rough terrain and remote areas all persons are advised to inform themselves of possible hazards due to man or wildlife. Campers should take all necessary precautions to ensure the safety and well-being of themselves and their group.

This book is dedicated to
my best friend,
camping buddy,
and wife
BRENDA

Acknowledgments

The author gratefully acknowleges the help and assistance of so many individuals who generously gave of their time and effort, especially Victor Brown, Jr., Blaine Yorgason, Robert Shawgo, Jr., the National Forest Service, Rip and Maralee Black, Doug and Peggy Cole, Jane Clayson, Linda Hunter Adams, and Karen Lusby.

And a special thanks to those who went on all those camps with me: my wife and our children—Matthew, Michael, Angela, and Brandon.

Contents

Introduction

THE IDEAL FAMILY OUTING

What's the first thing you think of when you hear the word "*camping*"? Pine trees? Lakes? Mountains? Bug repellant? Motels? When I mention camping in conversations with people, I'm often amused at all the definitions that come up. They range from backpacking in remote wilderness areas, to luxury motorhomes in a trailer park, and yes, even to motels. Some people can't stand the thought of being more than fifty feet from a restroom, while others want to get as far from civilization as possible. Many want to go, dreaming of rusticating in the pines, but back away from the idea because they're not sure *how* to prepare, *where* to go, or *what* to do, especially when they have children.

There's one viewpoint about camping that most people share: a camping trip is an escape, an opportunity to get away from it all.

Whether you take an RV or tent, this book will show you how to get the most out of what you want from your camping trips so that every member of the family can have a great time.

I can think of no other setting that breathes such rejuvenation into life than being in the primitive backyard of Mother Nature. Anything from peaceful relaxation to stimulating adventure is yours for the taking if you are *properly prepared* for it. Preparation is the key, and finding out what combination of camping styles fits your family's needs will be what makes *your* camp the most comfortable. Every family is different, and as you read through this book, you'll probably see methods that are to your liking and others that are not. Take plenty of notes and try different things to see what suits your family's tastes, and before long you'll have a tailored system for all your outdoor ventures.

Looking back on my youth, I recall many camping excursions I went on, either with my family or with a Boy Scout troop. Some were the most enjoyable moments of my life, while others made a high school algebra test more appealing.

After several camps, I could tell there was a big difference between what I did on the fun camps and what I did on the camps that made me wish I had never left home. It took some time before I finally figured out what I needed to do for *all* of those camps to be as much fun as I expected. Then when the children came along, I was back to experiencing a few camps that made me consider yard work as my preferred escape.

For some reason, I kept hanging onto this idea that there had to be some way to make camping trips equally enjoyable for every member of the family. I decided to set out on a lengthy crusade to find out what worked and what didn't. It took a few years of camping almost every month to "weed out" the things that didn't work. What remains is a collection of methods that have made camping our favorite family outing.

Fortunately, you don't have to go through the extremes we did; you can read this book, put the principles to work, and get it right the first time. This book will focus on the three main parts of a camping trip: before, during, and after. The first part, things you do before your camp, is the most important. I'm sure you'll agree that no matter how beautiful the scenery, how serene the setting, or how fantastic the fishing on your camping trip, it can all be spoiled by some discomfort caused by lack of preparation. The second part will deal with the things that you do on the way, at the camp, and on the way back. The last part explains the things you do when you get home that will help you make your next trip even better.

So turn the page and let's start planning *your* next trip.

Chapter I

WHERE TO GO

The first and most frequent question people ask me when they want to go camping is "Where's a good place to go?" Naturally, this is one of the most important considerations to have in mind. There's nothing more frustrating about a camping trip than to have a few precious days off work, drive to a supposed great spot to spend that time, and find that the area you sacrificed yourself for is a mosquito-infested swamp.

I used to pick new areas from a highway map marked with national forest boundaries. However, the maps can be misleading. I once took our family on a camping trip to what looked like a cool shady lake area in a national forest. We had high hopes of escaping a 108-degree July heatwave. When we arrived after a five-hour journey, the supposedly shady lake was surrounded by sagebrush, the heat was unbearable, and flies were everywhere. We were sick of driving, so we stayed and endured the miserable heat with a makeshift shade canopy.

On the other hand, we've driven to supposedly warm areas and found ourselves freezing in our tent because the temperature at night—even in July—dropped drastically.

The best favor you can do for yourself is to do a few minutes of telephone work before you leave. If you are new to the area, start with the state's travel council or travel commission. Many states have them, and they're prominently talked about in the preface pages of many telephone directories. These travel offices are very eager to answer questions about places to go, things to see, historic sites—you name it. Call, pay them a visit, or write them.

Your travel council is the best place to start.

When you visit your local travel council, you will most likely find it has more information about things to do and see in your

Places and places to visit!

Brochures for all your interests

state than anywhere else you can go, so load up on the free brochures and information. Also, be sure to ask for a list of the national forest offices in your local region. They will be extremely handy in your planning.

If you haven't been camping in the local region before, it is usually best to pick the national forest or camping area closest to home. You can find the phone number of the forest supervisor for a region through directory assistance.

If you are going to a national forest area or Bureau of Land Management (BLM) area, calling the forest supervisor or district office of that region will give you the advantage of talking to someone who is *at* the area you are visiting. Simply tell them that you're interested in camping in that area and ask them what places they would recommend. You might ask if there are lakes you can camp by, or if there is water available.

These offices are helpful in directing new travelers to good areas. I found them to be valuable for finding out if dirt roads had been washed out or closed. Some offices even have forest service travel maps they can send to you which show all roads in the unimproved areas, with detailed markings of road conditions, hazards, etc. A few offices have sent me maps free of charge; others required a small fee.

Among the considerations for vicariously "knowing" the area are elevation and climate. Although you may be experiencing balmy weather in June where you live, the higher elevation of a particular camping spot may have snow as late as August; so choose an area that has a climate that will suit your intentions. ALWAYS be prepared for extremely cold winter conditions when you venture into the outdoors—especially in the mountains. I've often seen hot August days in the canyons dip below freezing temperatures at night. This is always an important matter to discuss with a forest supervisor's office.

A good question to ask if you are planning to travel on unimproved roads is whether the road conditions are suitable for the particular vehicle you are driving. If you are embarking on your trip in a minivan or a four-passenger sedan, you'll want to avoid getting into four-wheel-drive roads that could send you home with damage to the undercarriage of your car. Not all mountain roads, speaking mainly of unimproved roads, require high chassis, four-wheel-drive capabilities. To date, I have never owned a four-wheel-drive vehicle and have taken only a passenger van or a two-wheel-drive pickup on all of my camps. Some roads are smooth enough for all types of automobiles—but find out first. The forest service office will likely know the roads and will give you their opinion about what roads you should or shouldn't drive on.

You can ask forest ranger offices for a description of the areas in which you wish to camp, such as if they have trees to pitch your tent under, or if there are mosquitoes that time of year, or what the fishing is like in the lake nearby.

I take my camping seriously, making calls and plans for a certain area a couple of weeks in advance, especially if I haven't been there before. Getting information about an area before you go will save you an incredible amount of trouble; you'll be adequately prepared for the conditions you'll encounter or be able to avoid certain areas altogether. If you have not camped in an area, I recommend trying the established campgrounds first, using them as base camps while you explore the surrounding area. The camp areas closest to you will be your best bet before you venture farther.

If possible, avoid going on your camps on major holidays. For most, camping is for getting away from people and congestion, but going camping on Memorial Day (which we never do) is like taking the entire state's population with you. There may be remote areas that you can find that are vacant, but you still have to contend with the traffic to and from the area.

One Memorial Day I was parked in the parking lot of a store near a freeway. I watched the deluge of campers and RVs pouring off the nearby exit ramp and could see the faces of the people from where I sat. They all looked so frazzled and nerve-racked from dealing with the traffic congestion that it confirmed my beliefs about not going anywhere on that holiday, or any holiday when the rest of the world goes camping.

To reduce the impact of high usage of forest areas, the National Forest Service also encourages campers to avoid camping on congested holidays.

Depending on where you live, there may be plenty of opportunities for camping during most of the year. Some folks limit their camping to the midsummer months, thus missing out on great camps in the spring or fall. We have a camping schedule that takes up most of the year.

If your state has an arid sector where deserts are common, therein lies a hidden treasure. Deserts are all too often stereotyped as wastelands. Thanks to a Scoutmaster who loved the desert, when I was a boy I learned to enjoy an aspect of nature that most people pass up.

The desert has a beauty of its own and can be enjoyed during the colder months when high elevations are restrictive. Many desert mountain formations are an adventure to explore.

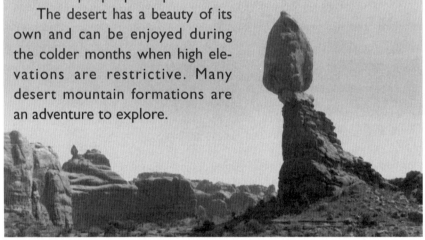

Deserts are best visited during cooler months.

Deserts can be fun to explore.

In October, we visit a popular lake in our state and find that we have most of the beaches to ourselves. The temperature is spring-like, and the water is warm. Most people have their vacations during the summer, when school is out, but if you take advantage of the school breaks, those short trips can really be fun. Areas where school is on a year-round basis allow frequent opportunities for camps throughout the year. I prefer several short trips myself, because when I come back from one trip, I don't have to wait a whole year for the next one.

Depending on what your schedule permits, you can frequently camp in popular areas at times when they are less crowded. Ask a ranger or someone from the area about the least crowded time of year so you can develop a strategy for the visit.

Notes

_____
_____
_____
_____
_____
_____
_____
_____
_____
_____
_____
_____
_____
_____
_____
_____
_____
_____
_____
_____
_____
_____
_____
_____
_____

Notes

_____

_____

_____

_____

_____

_____

_____

_____

_____

_____

_____

_____

_____

_____

_____

_____

_____

_____

_____

_____

_____

_____

_____

_____

_____

_____

Chapter 2

MAKE A PLAN

If you want to ensure that you make the most of every camping minute, invest some time before you leave and make a plan, or a general itinerary.

When you make your calls to find out what a certain camping area is like, you will probably think of things you will want to do in that area, such as fishing, hiking, mountain biking, exploring, and so on. Once you have an idea as to what is available at the camp area, you can discuss all of the preferred activities with your family. Some family members may want to fish, while others prefer hiking; others might want to nap.

Whatever the choices, make a list of them and, if possible, schedule in a fair amount of time for each one. Here's a simple plan:

were dressed, yet too embarrassed to climb out with our frazzled hair and hazy eyes. We decided to just open the curtains little by little and pretend we were spectators at the events with the best front row seats. We pulled it off—at least I like to think we did.

For obvious reasons, I make every effort to arrive at the campsite no later than mid-afternoon. If possible, your best assurance will be to leave home first thing in the morning.

Notes

Notes

_____

_____

_____

_____

_____

_____

_____

_____

_____

_____

_____

_____

_____

_____

_____

_____

_____

_____

_____

_____

_____

_____

_____

_____

_____

_____

Chapter 3

THE PACKING LIST

How many times have you left on vacation and just thirty seconds down the road you realize you forgot something? Or do you continually fret for the first few miles worrying that you may have forgotten something but don't know what?

I know the feeling well. In fact, I remember having to go back to our house four times on one trip—fortunately we were less than half a mile away each time.

Your packing list is perhaps the most valuable preparation tool you have. This list should be a master list that you make and take with you on the camp. While you are on your camp, you can write down the things you wish you had brought or done.

It took me several camps to perfect our list. Now when we leave, we never worry about whether this or that was packed because everything that we have ever concerned ourselves with is checked off.

This chapter contains inclusive lists of items you may want to consider bringing. Naturally, you won't want to take everything on each trip—it depends on the trip and on your needs. Some people prefer to take only what they can get by with; others take more. The balance between traveling light and being adequately equipped is different for everyone, so you should decide where your preferences fit in and what your tastes require. My own saying has been, "Take the least possible, but the most necessary."

Although the master list is long, most of the articles take up very little space, and many come in smaller sizes. Some items will have an explanation; take what you prefer and leave the rest.

You might find, as we have, that a small utility trailer is very handy for taking your camping gear, especially if you are driving a car, van, or other vehicle where packing space is limited.

Our camping list is divided into categories, or sections, for items that will be packed together.

The first section is about our "cooking box." We made ours from a secondhand luggage trunk, the lightweight kind that measure 12" x 15" x 30". I recommend getting some kind of closeable container for the cooking items so you can always leave your kitchen-type things packed in it. This will streamline your packing jobs in the future as all these items will be readily packed if you camp frequently. All you have to do is open the box, check off the articles on your list before you go, and throw the box on board. The items on the cooking box list comprise about one-fifth of the total.

The Cooking Box

Paper towels	Dish soap
Cooking oil	Spoons, forks, knives

Newspaper
Tongs
Whisk broom
Sandwich bags
Dishcloths and towels
Cutting board
Cooking apron
Scouring pad
Aluminum foil
Lg. serving utensils
Lg. cutting knives
Paper, pencils, tape
Fly swatter
Matches

Steak knives
Cups or paper cups
Plates or paper plates
Garbage bags
Plastic pitcher
Salt & pepper
Knife sharpener
Small fire extinguisher
Measuring spoons & cups
Can opener
Sauce pan(s)
Lg. pot (heating water)
Storage containers
Hot pads

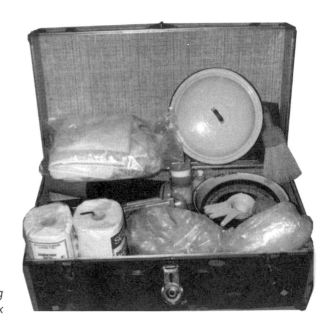

*The cooking
box*

You may have items you want to add to your cooking box besides this, or you may want to take fewer, depending on if you like to cook in the outdoors or feast on prepared, take-out food. We make a complete and separate meal list, or a menu, and from it I list all the ingredients that need to be packed in the cooler or food box. These items are all packed separately. Things needing refrigeration go in the cooler; the rest can simply be packed in an appropriately sized cardboard box or container of your choice.

The second section describes our "bathroom box," a plastic container no bigger than a medium-sized cardboard box. It contains all the toiletries that your family may need on the trip. It also contains all medications and some first-aid supplies.

The Bathroom Box

Bar or liquid soap	Cough syrup
Shampoo	Petroleum jelly
Toilet paper	Razor (opt)
Curling iron (opt)	Deodorant
Toothpaste	Toothbrushes
Dental floss	Mouthwash
Sun block	Burn medication
Suntan lotion	Hayfever medication
Snakebite kit (or bee sting)	Vaporizing rub
Cotton balls	Hand lotion
Clothespins	Insect repellant
Children's aspirin	Pain reliever
Make-up (opt)	Fingernail clippers
Combs, brushes	Cough drops
Talcum powder	Bandages
Feminine products	Laundry bag
Upset stomach remedy	Bath cloths and towels

The bathroom box

The bathroom box section of the list was compiled and added to while we were *on* camps and includes things we wished we had at different times but forgot to pack. You'll be glad you packed them too, when your youngest child wakes up at 2 AM with a cough or sore throat and you're able to treat it and go on with your camp. Otherwise, one sick family member can shorten the enjoyment for everyone. Even when I am backpacking, I always take miniature containers for unexpected ailments.

The beauty of the bathroom and cooking boxes is that they can be packed well in advance without any problem and stored in a convenient out-of-the-way place at home until it's time to load up. If you plan to camp frequently, you may want to buy supplies specifically for camping, such as inexpensive plastic dishes and so forth, and leave them packed.

The third section of the list is for main items such as the tent and the equipment.

Main Items

Tent

Tent stakes

Screen tent

Water containers

Spare motor oil

Games

Binoculars (opt)

Tools

Fishing gear

Firewood

Rope & wire

Blankets

Ice

Tent heater

Shovel

Mattress pump (opt)

Stove

Folding chairs

Cooler or ice chest

Auto tire compressor

Lantern

Fire pan

Doormat

Tent rug

Table

Camera & extra film

Cash

Hatchet or ax

Sink or tub

Fishing licenses

Fishing bait

Toilet stall

Sleeping bags

Pillows

Ice water

Toilet & chemicals

Mattress pads

Winch, tow chain & rod

Stove fuel

Saw

Small broom

Life jackets

Dutch oven

Dutch oven equipment

Now a few words about some of the main articles.

The tent: I don't think it's always necessary to buy "hi-tech" equipment, but if you plan on going camping more than once or twice a year, I suggest investing in the tent—it will be well worth the money.

Our family's tents are made out of heavy duty marine canvas and are rated to withstand a 90-mile-per-hour wind, and are waterproof as well.

One summer, we were camping on the shores of Lake Powell, on the Utah–Arizona border, when a fierce electrical storm came up in the middle of the night. Weather reports indicated that there were gusts up to 70 miles per hour. The shore was crowded with hundreds of campers, RVs, and tents when thunder pounded the surrounding area. As we cowered in our sleeping bags, we watched the sides of the tent bow in toward us. We could hear the "clank" sounds of nearby tents collapsing in the relentless winds and the yelling of the people inside them while they climbed out of the mess and ran for their cars.

When the tent next to us collapsed, we could hear people yelling to each other to grab this or that item as they ran to their car. We then heard a small girl's voice asking her mother, "Why isn't their tent blowing down, Mommy?" At that instant my wife and I turned and looked at each other, grinning, and I said: "This would make a great commercial for the company that made this tent!"

We spent a considerable sum of money on our tent, and that night it was worth every penny. Not a drop of rain got on our bedding, and strangely enough our kids never woke up. The next morning, our tent was the only one standing.

Check around and find out who manufactures tents in your area and see how they are rated. You may pay extra for the quality, but when Mother Nature unleashes her temper, you'll be glad you have a strong piece of equipment protecting you.

I would also suggest that you buy a tent that is large and roomy. Our largest tent measures 10' x 14'. Not only is the spaciousness good for sleeping, but if inclement weather forces you inside, it's nice to have a place of retreat bigger than a pup tent.

If you have an average or large size family like we do, an additional pup tent for the older kids not only gives Mom and Dad a little more privacy but a quieter night's sleep as well.

Be sure to take along a ground cover to put under the tent, such as a plastic or canvas tarp, to protect the bottom of the tent. It keeps the tent cleaner, too.

Rubber doormat: Nice to have when shoes encounter some mud.

Tent rug: The rug goes inside and helps to minimize wear on the floor of your tent. It also makes a comfortable surface to walk on at night with bare feet.

Tent stakes: I recommend that you have a couple of types of tent stakes in your camp storage, to use depending on the terrain where you will be camping. When we bought our tent, it came with space-age plastic tent stakes, guaranteed not to break. When we got our tent home, I set it up on the back lawn and broke the third stake I put in the grass. No rocks, just weak plastic, I suppose. So carry spares.

That thunderstorm I told you about was one I was prepared for. Someone had warned me about summer storms and sandy beaches, so I took along some 18" stakes developed for use in sand. The stakes were one of the main reasons our tent didn't blow down.

Another type of tent stake I recommend is an old railroad spike. Some mountains we have camped on had soil so rocky that we would have been doomed if it weren't for these spikes. They are literally indestructible and come in handy in the event your plastic stake hits a rock. An old army ammo box makes a great carrier for these spikes. The spikes can be found in some salvage yards or railroad supply stores.

Screen tent or dining tent: Nothing more than a tent with walls made of screening material, this tent was the answer to a lot of problems we had on tent camps, and you'll love it too. Of all the complaints I've heard or experienced on tent camps, the most frequent are about bugs, flies, and mosquitoes. Even with a great mosquito repellent, when you sit down to eat, the bugs come too—and you can't put repellent on your food. A dining tent solves the problem. Not only does this handy item keep us from the bugs, but it's a fantastic shade canopy on a hot day. If we take mountain bikes along, the screen tent is an excellent carport to put the bikes under. If you have a baby or toddler who wants to wander off from time to time, the screen tent is a wonderful solution as a playpen. You can keep a little tyke safely zipped up inside, and he or she has plenty of room to play. A piece of outdoor patio turf cut to size for the floor makes this even better for a little one. The uses are endless.

Since such tents are made of delicate window screening all the way around, a tear will most likely develop from time to time. Keep a small sewing kit with the tent for minor repairs.

I recommend buying a screen tent from a place that sells used or refurbished tents. The new ones we looked at cost around $250. I found a good refurbished one for $60 and it works great. It had a few patches, but the mosquitoes didn't seem to notice—they missed dinner and us, anyway!

Fold-up table: The best table and chair invention of late is a plastic fold-up type. It has four bench seats which fold up inside the table, and then the whole thing folds up to the size of a long suitcase. My favorite trinkets are things that fold up from a maximum use size to a compact easy-carry size. This table is available in many hardware and sporting goods stores and currently sells for around $50.

Water carrier(s): This is an important piece of equipment, and, surprisingly, the most commonly forgotten or underestimated. The handiest thing we have found to carry water is the square five-gallon plastic water jugs that have an on/off spout. How much water to take depends on how long you will stay, what you plan to do with it, and whether fresh water is available at the campsite.

I've noticed over the years how much more water we've had to cart along with us as our family has grown. You might say that you'd prefer to get yours out of the closest stream or lake. I strongly caution you **NOT** to do this. You never know what is upstream that could be contaminating the water. A real danger in drinking from mountain streams exists, as there is always the strong possibility of a dead animal or other contaminating source that could cause you to become infected with parasites, some of which you can never get rid of.

Your usage may contaminate the water downstream. I've seen individuals wash things, with soap, in the nearest stream or dump their waste water in the current, not considering the wildlife that drink, not to mention **live**, in the downstream area. Bring your own water or an adequate filtration system, and dispose of it away from waterways.

Camera and extra film: The family memories which you've captured on film will be the greatest of treasures from your experiences outdoors. Our children spend hours of laughter looking at the volumes of photos we've taken when they were younger. Some photo shops sell disposable cameras with pre-packed film. We use these when we camp in areas where it might be hazardous to take an expensive camera.

Extra motor oil: Check your oil upon arrival at your campsite; steep grades up a canyon can cause your engine to consume more oil than usual.

Cash: Take a reasonable amount of cash along and have more than one person carry it. Having extra money in case of unexpected surprises can really get you out of a jam. A credit card is also handy for emergencies.

Games: Come in handy in inclement weather.

Hatchet: Good for splitting small firewood.

Binoculars: An optional "toy."

Plastic sink or small tub: For washing in general.

Tools: Hammer, screwdrivers, pliers, wrenches, etc. If a piece of your camping equipment breaks, or your vehicle has a problem, it's nice to be able to remedy the situation.

Fishing licenses and fishing gear: If you plan to do some fishing, don't forget your license. It surprises me to hear news reports of how many people try to fish without their license because they forgot to bring it along. Since this is not a book about fishing, I will simply suggest that you provide for the children simple gear that you're not afraid to lose. Once while in a boat, our oldest son cast his line beautifully out into the lake . . . and along with it went the rod.

Fishing bait: This has been known to be left behind at times.

Fire pan: (Or table-top barbecue) Great to have along to keep from leaving fire ring scars, for use with your Dutch oven, or in an inverted position as a cover for Dutch ovens. I'll talk more about Dutch ovens in chapter 6.

Firewood: Taking your own firewood along is much easier than hacking up the forest trying to find dry wood.

Privacy "tent" or bathroom stall: This is a narrow stand-up tent, sometimes sold as a stall or shower tent in sporting goods stores. If this fits your liking in the camping process, take it along, especially if you have company.

Rope and wire: I cannot count the number of times I've needed rope to hang up something to dry or a piece of wire to fix various things, so take along a roll of medium-sized rope and some light tie wire.

Sleeping bags: One of the mistakes we made at the outset was going to the store to buy "just a sleeping bag" for our trips. I had no idea at the time that sleeping bags came with different temperature ratings, so it was no wonder we were badly chilled on some of our first camps.

I took comfort in knowing other people who had taken Dad's hand-me-down bag and have had the same experience. Buying the cheapest sleeping bag on the shelf as I did will leave you regretting it as your family's teeth chatter like a castanet band.

My "school of hard knocks" education has led me to find out that there are varying temperature ratings on most sleeping bags sold. If there is *not* a rating on the bag you are thinking of buying, don't buy it—quality sleeping bags will openly display temperature ratings. After I learned this, I was really surprised to return to the store where we bought ours and saw that the same ones we had were rated for "cool" conditions. Whoops!

The colder protection rating bags next on the shelf were rated for moderate conditions, only down to just above freezing. I couldn't find anything rated for below freezing conditions, and such a bag is necessary most of the time in canyons and mountains.

Most sporting goods stores carry a wide variety of all types and ratings of bags. Without getting into the high-tech-several-hundred-dollar bags, many fall into a reasonable dollar range yet offer ample protection from the cold.

The rating of a sleeping bag largely depends on how much inner filling it has and what kind. Every year, manufacturers produce bags with more insulative materials that are lighter in weight and offer maximum protection. Goose down is the finest unless it gets wet or damp, but is also very costly. Most of the new synthetic fibers used today closely mimic the effect of down and cost much less.

If you don't know what your sleeping bags are rated for, take one of them into a camping supply store that sells hi-tech gear and ask their opinion. Then you can decide if the conditions you will be camping in warrant a new purchase. Otherwise, take a few dozen blankets.

We feel that it is best to be prepared for the worst; all our sleeping bags are rated for cold situations of zero degrees or colder.

Blankets: Another thing you can do to be safe in night temperatures is take along some good blankets. We always pack them along to pad under our sleeping bags and at times on top of them for added comfort or warmth.

The blankets we take camping were purchased for $3 each at a thrift store, so we're not afraid to take them where they encounter the elements.

Cooler or ice chest: This is pretty much up to you as to the size and quality; shop around until you find the right size cooler or ice chest. Fill any extra space with wadded up newspapers to extend the life of your ice and to keep things colder longer.

Ice: We've tried block, crushed, and dry ice. The least expensive and longest lasting method we've found is to fill empty plastic milk jugs and keep them in the freezer. We usually have about three on hand, and they are convenient to use in our cooler. With the lids on the jugs, they don't leak and can be put right back in the freezer when we get home. Best of all, the jugs are free.

Ice water: For convenience and thirst quenching, we keep a jug of ice water and cups in the vehicle while we're traveling.

Heater: We have found a few non-electric space heaters that are very nice to have along, especially in a tent while getting dressed on a cold morning. These types of heaters use either white fuel or propane, and both models I've used put out 3,000 BTUs. Using space heaters in tents can be risky, especially around children, so take all precautions recommended by the manufacturers, and be careful how you use them. Be sure that your tent is large enough to accommodate a heater and that you always allow adequate ventilation.

Buy your heater from a reputable dealer who can properly instruct you as to its use with your individual set-up.

Chemical toilet: This is handy to have along if a lot of company will be around you, and it aspires to the highest of environmental standards. A chemical toilet is also very convenient. I'll address this and other environmental concerns in more detail in chapter 8.

Shovel: A small fold-up shovel is convenient and a good idea to always keep in your vehicle.

Air mattresses or pads: To keep your back from being sore all night from sleeping on the ground, take these along. If space permits, I prefer foam pads, but they are bulky to pack it you have a lot of gear. Several types of pads are available—choose the ones you like best. We use the roll-up/self-inflating pads most of the time. If you take an air mattress, remember to pack the inflator!

Winch, tow chain, and rod: I have been stuck enough times to know the value of having this collection in my vehicle. A rod or stake allows you an anchor to hook the winch to in case there are no trees, such as on a sandy beach. A tow chain is essential for the job, as well as helping someone else being towed.

Stove: A white fuel stove is handy for a quick heating job, such as hot water or for cooking quick and easy meals.

Stove or heater fuel: Carry an extra can of fuel along for your stove or heater. Keep it stored in a cool safe place.

Folding chairs: An extra luxury for sitting around the fire or looking at the stars.

Saw: If you use wood branches for firewood, a saw will come in handy.

Pillows: These should be packed in a bag of some type, to keep them from getting dusty if you travel on dirt roads.

Small broom: Great for sweeping out the tent.

Small tire compressor: If you spring a leak in a tire, especially the spare, a few minutes with the compressor and you'll be rolling again.

Life jackets: These are as necessary for being around water as seat belts are for motorists. Whether or not we plan on boating, we take life jackets for any area where we know we will be near water. Drownings happen every year from little ones falling into rivers, streams, and even irrigation ditches. Have your children wear a life jacket if they play near water, and you will be more at ease.

Lantern: A heavy-duty light source such as a white fuel or gas lantern makes the nighttime camp area safer and much more pleasant.

The fourth section is for personal items such as each person's clothes, packed in his or her own duffel bag. You can purchase medium-sized duffel bags for each person in the family. We all have different colored bags, and in them go our clothes, pillow, and personal things.

Personal Items

Caps and hats	Swimsuit
Coats	Gloves
Hiking boots/outdoor shoes	Clothing, underwear
Fanny pack	Pocket knife

When you pack for the children, pack clothing you will not worry about, and let the kids have fun. Smaller children have fun getting a little dirty, but we sometimes fret over them staying clean and out of the elements. Camping should be a time that you let go and let them feel a bit of creative freedom. It won't hurt a thing. We always pack two days' worth of extra clothes so it won't be a problem if the children get wet or dirty.

As with the sleeping bags, your coats and hats should be of good quality. Having been on many winter camps in sub-zero temperatures, I have come to the conclusion that there is no reason a person has to be cold. Air is the best insulator, and insulative fibers that create a good air space in clothing are the best for colder weather. Again, be sure to pack winter clothing and coats even in July if you are venturing to higher elevations. Ordinarily, wear what you feel most comfortable in, but having the appropriate clothing along for all conditions will ensure your comfort.

The fifth section is for items to have out and accessible while driving.

Up Front in the Vehicle

Book tapes	Flashlights/batteries
First-aid kit	Travel information
Food or snacks	Kids' travel kits (see chapter 4)

Book tapes: How would you like to have your kids sit quietly and without moving in the back seat of your vehicle for an hour? You can: just check out storybook tapes at the local library, play them on your cassette deck or portable tape player, and the kids will be in a trance the whole time while they read along. We checked out eight tape-stories once to cover the entire length of the trip. Or, if your budget allows, a portable TV with a videotape player takes the kids' minds off the travel tedium with a movie. We do this at times, and judge some of our travel distances by how many movies they will have to watch before we arrive. Our children seem to understand that concept better than "we'll get there in four hours."

First-aid kit: In a later chapter, I will list suggested items you can put in your first-aid kit if you want to make one, or you can buy one. Homemade ones, I think, are better, but no matter which route you choose, always have one.

Flashlights and spare batteries: Have at least one flashlight per family member. Keep the batteries out of them during storage in case they leak.

Travel information, brochures, and maps: If you plan to make stops at points of interest along the way, travel materials will facilitate finding them. They will also help you find your destination.

The final section is for things we need to do around the house before we leave, such as leaving lights on or turning the heat down.

Before Leaving

Arrange for pet care	Secure doors and windows
Turn heat down	Shut off water

An insurance agent once told me that more house floods occur from ruptured washing machine hoses than from any other cause. And if you have any pranksters in your neighborhood, it will be less of a thrill to them when they turn your garden hose on and nothing happens—if you've shut off the appropriate water valve before you left. To keep water pipes from bursting in cold weather, turn heat no lower than 55°. If you will be gone more than two or three days, take safety precautions such as leaving a radio and lights on.

If you are taking any sporting equipment, such as a boat or mountain bikes, make a tailored list, including life jackets, helmets, or other items specific for your preferences and destination.

The old adage "the right tool for the right job" applies to life in the outdoors.

Now let's put it all together. This is what the full list should look like:

MASTER CAMPING LIST

The Cooking Box:

- ❏ Paper towels
- ❏ Cooking oil
- ❏ Newspaper
- ❏ Tongs
- ❏ Whisk broom
- ❏ Sandwich bags
- ❏ Dishcloths and towels
- ❏ Cutting board
- ❏ Cooking apron
- ❏ Scouring pad
- ❏ Aluminum foil
- ❏ Lg. serving utensils
- ❏ Lg. cutting knives
- ❏ Paper, pencils, tape
- ❏ Fly swatter
- ❏ Matches
- ❏ _____
- ❏ _____
- ❏ _____

- ❏ Dish soap
- ❏ Spoons, forks, knives
- ❏ Steak knives
- ❏ Cups or paper cups
- ❏ Plates or paper plates
- ❏ Garbage bags
- ❏ Plastic pitcher
- ❏ Salt & pepper
- ❏ Knife sharpener
- ❏ Small fire extinguisher
- ❏ Measuring spoons & cups
- ❏ Can opener
- ❏ Sauce pan(s)
- ❏ Lg. pot (heating water)
- ❏ Storage containers
- ❏ Hot pad(s)
- ❏ _____
- ❏ _____
- ❏ _____

The Bathroom Box:

- ❏ Bar or liquid soap
- ❏ Shampoo
- ❏ Toilet paper
- ❏ Curling iron (opt)
- ❏ Toothpaste
- ❏ Dental floss
- ❏ Sun block
- ❏ Suntan lotion

- ❏ Cough syrup
- ❏ Petroleum jelly
- ❏ Razor (opt)
- ❏ Deodorant
- ❏ Toothbrushes
- ❏ Mouthwash
- ❏ Burn medication
- ❏ Hayfever medication

❏ Snakebite kit (or bee sting)
❏ Cotton balls
❏ Clothespins
❏ Children's aspirin
❏ Make-up (opt)
❏ Combs, brushes
❏ Talcum powder
❏ Feminine products
❏ Upset stomach remedies
❏ _____
❏ _____

❏ Vaporizing rub
❏ Hand lotion
❏ Insect repellant
❏ Pain reliever
❏ Fingernail clippers
❏ Cough drops
❏ Bandages
❏ Laundry bag
❏ Bath cloths and towels
❏ _____
❏ _____

Main Items:

❏ Tent
❏ Tent stakes
❏ Screen tent
❏ Water containers
❏ Spare motor oil
❏ Games
❏ Binoculars (opt)
❏ Tools
❏ Fishing gear
❏ Firewood
❏ Rope & wire
❏ Blankets
❏ Ice
❏ Tent heater
❏ Shovel
❏ Mattress pump (opt)
❏ Stove
❏ Folding chairs
❏ Cooler or ice chest

❏ Doormat
❏ Tent rug
❏ Table
❏ Camera & extra film
❏ Cash
❏ Hatchet or ax
❏ Sink or tub
❏ Fishing licenses
❏ Fishing bait
❏ Toilet stall
❏ Sleeping bags
❏ Pillows
❏ Ice water
❏ Toilet & chemicals
❏ Mattress pads
❏ Winch, tow chain & rod
❏ Stove fuel
❏ Saw
❏ Small broom

- ❏ Auto tire compressor
- ❏ Lantern
- ❏ Fire pan
- ❏ _____
- ❏ _____

- ❏ Life jackets
- ❏ Dutch oven
- ❏ Dutch oven equipment
- ❏ _____
- ❏ _____

Personal Items:

- ❏ Caps & hats
- ❏ Coats
- ❏ Hiking boots/outdoor shoes
- ❏ Fanny pack
- ❏ _____
- ❏ _____

- ❏ Swimsuit
- ❏ Gloves
- ❏ Clothing, underwear
- ❏ Pocket knife
- ❏ _____
- ❏ _____

Up Front in Vehicle:

- ❏ Book tapes
- ❏ First-aid kit
- ❏ Food or snacks
- ❏ _____
- ❏ _____

- ❏ Flashlights/batteries
- ❏ Travel information
- ❏ Kids' travel kits
- ❏ _____
- ❏ _____

Before Leaving:

- ❏ Feed pets
- ❏ Turn heat down
- ❏ _____
- ❏ _____

- ❏ Secure doors/windows
- ❏ Shut off water
- ❏ _____
- ❏ _____

One additional checklist should be noted here. The last place you want to have an engine failure is on your camping trip, miles from home in the middle of nowhere. The engine in your vehicle will strain harder on your journey to the mountains due to steeper terrain and possibly rougher roads than what you usually drive on.

It is important that your maintenance is up to date to reduce the possibilities of breaking down.

Not a good place for a breakdown.

You should have your vehicle in top running condition before going to remote areas, especially if an emergency happens that requires driving to get medical help. This book is on camping, so I won't dwell on car maintenance; just be sure you know your car's needs and have a good spare tire, fan belt, and supplies.

Notes

Chapter 4

ALONG THE WAY

If there's one thing that can test a family's relationship it's being confined together in a car on a long trip. After we've traveled several miles in our van, the dialogue from the back seats goes something like this:

"Quit touching me."

"That's mine—give it back!"

"You're in my spot."

"Daaaad! He's looking at me!"

"Moooom, he took my toy."

And on and on.

Kids. I love mine dearly but question my reasoning for a vacation thirty minutes down the road when the clan starts picking on each other.

When seat belt laws came into effect, it was a challenge for us to keep our youngest ones convinced that the strap holding them hostage against the back seat might save their lives one day. On the freeway, the kids would unsnap the seat belt and crawl around unnoticed.

Keeping a child's attention absorbed and focused was our great quest to make traveling more enjoyable as well as safer. We eventually found some nifty ideas that really work and have put them to use. Even with the best of ideas, there are some occasions when the kids have a squabble or two, but nothing like it used to be.

The most effective tool, if money permits, is a portable TV/ VCR. The kids stay glued in their seat belts while Disney keeps them entertained. They even have a better concept of traveling time with movies because they seem to know how long a movie is better than what an hour is. Before, when they would whine, "How long before we get there?" it didn't matter if I said one hour or three, it was an eternity to them. With the TV, my reply is, "We'll get there in two movies." That they seem to understand.

Before we had money to buy the TV, we had a much more economical method that we still use and that works almost as well. As mentioned in the previous chapter, we check out storybook tapes from the local library and play them on our tape deck. While the kids read along and look at the pictures, we can drive in peace. The only drawback is that some of the tapes are not very long. They'll allow parents about five to ten minutes of safe driving in peace, so you may have to check out a *stack* of tapes as we have done.

Another invention that must be credited to my wife is the travel kit. She bought some small plastic cases from a closeout store and labeled one for each child. The cases were then filled with all kinds of toys, playthings, trinkets, books, notepads, pencils, color pencils, crayons, travel games or crafts, handheld video games, and car games. My wife also collects word puzzles from magazines and puts them in the kit.

The secret to making the travel kit entertaining is to let the kids have the contents of these kits only when they are on a trip. If they just have the things they always play with, they quickly lose interest. If reserved until the trip, the items inside the kits are fresh and new, and hold children's attention longer.

I must admit that the children aren't the only ones who get bored on trips. Obviously, we adults need a break as well. I've even felt cheated out of a sizeable portion of some of our camping trips largely because of the time invested in going long distances from home.

I discussed in chapter 2 how short camps are more beneficial when closer to home. A longer trip is warranted, however, when the destination is a special location, such as a family reunion, a scenic attraction, or a certain type of fishing. In such cases, we decided to find as many ways as possible to make the journey to and from our destination as enjoyable as the camp itself.

We sought historical markers as convenient

Historical markers are excellent places to take a break from driving.

Visitors' centers offer educational as well as travel diversions.

Ghost town sites are interesting and fun to visit.

and interesting places to stretch our legs. We were more interested in the adventurous stories than we originally thought we'd be. The stories have also helped us to appreciate the things so many people went through to make our lives better today.

We also found that ghost towns are fun to explore and old sites are photogenic. One of my favorite things to do on our trips ended up a new hobby—visiting ghost towns.

I happened upon a book about ghost towns in my state and found the stories in them absolutely fascinating. Along with the pictures in the book, there were sketched roads with landmarks to show where they once were.

Since then, we pick one town to visit on the way to our camp and one on the way back. My wife reads the story aloud as we are nearing the site, and it is like going on a guided tour. This doesn't take much time to do, especially if it's on the way, and allows us to stretch our legs.

Another idea is to visit any local attraction in one of those small towns you buzz through. One quaint little town had a cheese factory in it, so we spent thirty minutes while a guide took our family on a personal tour. The kids learned how cheese was made, and they tried some fresh cheese curd. They found it amusing how cheese curd squeaks against their teeth. Since it was like chewing a pencil eraser, they named it "eraser cheese." Each time we pass through that particular town, the children always ask, "Can we get some more eraser cheese, please?"

The travel brochures you acquire, as discussed in chapter 1, should offer many places you can visit throughout the regions you travel, so don't forget to take them along.

I know of people who race to get to their vacation destination and race back. Their family members often comment on how stressful their trips are, and it's no wonder. They need a vacation to rest from their vacation! Slowing down to enjoy life should start the minute you hop in the driver's seat and leave. Just be sure to allow plenty of time for the journey. Smell the roses along the way, live your vacation to the fullest, and the trip will be much more palatable to you as well as to the passengers in the back.

Makes a good break from a long trip.

Notes

_____
_____
_____
_____
_____
_____
_____
_____
_____
_____
_____
_____
_____
_____
_____
_____
_____
_____
_____
_____
_____
_____
_____
_____
_____

Notes

_____

_____

_____

_____

_____

_____

_____

_____

_____

_____

_____

_____

_____

_____

_____

_____

_____

_____

_____

_____

_____

_____

_____

_____

_____

_____

Chapter 5

CAMP SET-UP

When the family van stops at our camps, the passenger doors always explode open as though they are under pressure. We have four children, and as fast as they scatter in the new campground, it would appear as though we had twenty. This is when the family scouts out the area before we do any unpacking. It's a good idea to make sure the campsite is habitable, so you don't go to a lot of work for nothing. Things to look for are safety hazards, such as cliffs or places where a child could fall, massive ant colonies, dead animals, quicksand, deep water, cactus plants, or a visiting rock 'n' roll group.

If there are other campers in the area, be considerate of the strong possibility that they came on their camp for solitude, as most campers do. Nothing is more frustrating on a serene camp than to have a loud group of people pull up and camp next to your family and destroy the serenity of the surroundings. And it's even worse if they bring along an obnoxious dog.

In some forest areas where primitive camping is allowed, campers are not permitted to camp within 200 feet of each other, both for the privacy of other campers and for the environment. I always try to camp as far away from other campers as possible, so as not to invade their privacy and to feel more at ease about the noise my own children may create.

When you drive into the campsite, position your vehicle in a direction that would protect your family in case the vehicle fell out of gear and rolled. I've heard tragic news reports of the family car rolling during the night into the tent in which family members were sleeping, causing deaths and injuries.

I can relate to this story but was fortunate enough not to have any injuries to speak of. On one of our trips, I decided to nap one afternoon in the back of our camper van with one of our toddler-age boys. The rest of the family was out for a walk when I dozed off.

Suddenly, I felt the bed in our van jerk and start shaking. With sleepy eyes I sat up to see the scenery moving outside the window. The ignition key was not in "locked" position and our little boy had managed to pull the gearshift out of "park." While the van rolled backwards, I threw myself with adrenaline-powered speed to the front of the van and shoved the gearshift into park while pushing on the brake pedal with my hand. The van skidded to a stop twenty feet before going off a steep embankment, preventing an accident that could have been tragic.

The best and most vivid lessons we learn in life are the things *not* to do. This was one of those lessons. Since that day, when we park at a campsite, I face our vehicle toward a tree, or turn the wheels to face a hill in case of a roll-away accident. In addition, a couple of large rocks in front and behind the tires provide more insurance. Always consider the consequences of how and where you park.

If the place checks out, begin by dividing the set-up responsibilities. This is the best time for a parent to spend some constructive "one on one" with a child and to distribute the responsibilities to each family member.

The first item to be set up is the tent. Normally, the littlest child helps Daddy with this responsibility by carrying the pouch of tent stakes around, handing them to Dad as they are needed.

Placing the tent entails some important considerations. First, try to determine where water runoff would be if it rained. If you pitch your tent in a lower gulley area, you might find yourself taking a midnight swim if a thundershower hits. Ridge areas where the ground is level or slightly sloped have proven to be the best for us. The forest service also recommends that tents be staked away from waterways. Do not dig water barriers or trenches around tents.

Another important consideration for a good tent spot is the sun. When we first arrive in a camp area, I sometimes find myself turned around, not knowing which way is east or west. (This is a good reason to add a compass to your packing list.) Tents can get very warm in direct sunlight and thus unbearable to be in during the day. I always try to position our tent so that it catches the first rays of the morning sun on the east side of a group of trees. This way the tent can be warmed quickly after a cold night, then shaded during the rest of the day.

If you don't have a compass, you can make a solar compass by poking a very straight stick in the ground, pointing directly at the sun so there is no shadow. A short while later, when the sun moves, the shadow made by the stick will point directly to the east.

If you have a new tent, it will probably come with instructions on how to set it up. If I am using a tent for the first time, I find it helpful to assemble it on my back lawn before I leave, so I don't have any unforeseen surprises at the camp. If the tent has a complicated assembly, it may help to mark the ends of the tent poles with masking tape and permanent marker with letters or numbers to correspond with other marks on the tent or adjoining poles. This will help you to easily recognize where they go when you set it up at camp.

My wife has always taken the time to laminate related instruction sheets that belong to some of our equipment and then to attach them to the bag or case in some way. This elimates the risk of intruction sheets becoming torn or lost.

We've often had friends or relatives along who have borrowed tents from other people. It's amazing to me how many times they casually remarked as they unloaded that they hoped all the parts

Home, sweet home

were there. The majority of those times have been frustrating to them in that there *were* missing parts. A remote location far from home is the worst place to discover you're unprepared—especially with the tent.

Once the tent is set up, we begin setting up the inside while the older children carry supplies from the van. We determine where the beds will go, lay down any floor mats or outdoor shoe mats. An outdoor "welcome mat" will spare your bedding and equipment unnecessary dirt if shoes are cleaned or even taken off before you enter the tent. We use a small roll-up mat, along with rubber-backed carpet pads on the inside of our tents. This plan protects the inside floor of the tent and makes a nice "homey" feeling inside. You may not appreciate that feeling until the sun starts to set and you need a comfortable place of retreat.

We place a small fold-out table with attached seats inside the tent, off to one side, where we can sit and eat or play games if bad weather comes up. It's also nice to have a table to sit at for those members of our family who have special needs like taking out contact lenses.

We set up our beds with the pillow end at the highest point of the slope; otherwise, we'd all have headaches in the morning. If you anticipate frigid temperatures during the night, it's a good idea to have your head away from the tent wall while you sleep—the top of your head will be cold all night if you do. We found that if the pillow end of the bed has to be near a wall, a rolled up blanket or other barrier above the pillow shields the tops of our heads from the cold wall of the tent. Moisture condensation will also gather on the inside of tent walls in damp weather, leaving wet spots on sleeping bags if they touch the wall during the night.

I could never figure out where all that drippy moisture came from that collects on the inside of tent walls during the night, until I did some studies on winter camping. Sometimes it's from the moisture we breathe out of our lungs all night. A simple remedy is to make sure the top of a zippered window is slightly open to allow most of the moisture to escape. Moisture condensation can still accumulate—even if all the windows and door flaps are open—but not nearly as much.

If dinner is a ways off, we take a walk to scout out the further reaches of our temporary "neighborhood." For babies, we use a baby carrier that works like a back pack.

If we are having a campfire, our children's favorite task is building it. The fire pit is set down and a wood "teepee" is built in it, with small dry tinder or newspaper to start it. It always intrigues me to watch how our children are mesmerized by a campfire. They love to put twigs and other articles in it from time to time and need to be supervised closely.

Campfires make a great gathering place.

A tetherball game with paddles goes anywhere

If your children become bored, a treasure hunt is always a sure pleaser. This would require one of the parents sneaking away alone with a treat or small gift of some kind for each of the children. Place the "treasure" in a place that has a significant landmark, such as near a large tree or rock. Make little hints on small pieces of paper and hide them, creating a trail of clues, leading from one to the other, leading up to the treasure. Make as many hints and hide them for as long as you want the kids to be entertained, or for as long as you think their patience will hold up.

A paddleball game on a tether pole is the handiest of any confineable game. Games like baseball are not a good idea in a forest area, because a home run hit or fly ball would stand a poor chance of being found again, not to mention the trampling down of forest vegetation to find it.

Another idea is to obtain a book about plants in your region and then to see how many plants you can identify. This idea is very educational for the children as well as the parents.

I think that most small children are easily entertained by the outdoors. On some of our stops in remote areas along the way, I've noticed our children always finding things to do, even in sagebrush. They always manage to find a pretty rock ("pretty" by their standards), or a "dinosaur bone," or other imaginative souvenirs that end up cluttering the floor of the van. Since children are naturally curious, don't be afraid to let go and watch them explore their surroundings.

We used to trouble ourselves about the children getting dirty, but as time went on, we found that letting our children get their hands dirty while playing was part of their having fun. Dressing our children in clothes that were set aside for outdoor playing aided this effort. With this in mind, our parental stress about separation from the elements became less of a full-time concern. There was always the opportunity to wash up in our little sink, and the facilities for a sponge bath if necessary.

Even if your sons or daughters are not in a Scouting program, the Scouting-type handbooks offer several outdoor ideas that are fun for children of all ages. Most bookstores carry these or can get one for you.

If you feel that there might be a risk of your children wandering too far and getting lost, you may want to purchase some strong whistles and attach them with a string to their shirt button for them to blow on if they become lost.

Take along some games to play at a table, in the event a storm comes up. Inside our tent and at a small table, we play board games or similar activities that involve the entire family. Coloring books with crayons are fun for the smaller children, too.

One of the determining factors for locations where we like to go camping is fishing. Each of our children is equipped with his or her own miniature tackle box and a small, easy-to-handle fishing pole. Water is a great entertainer for our children. When they were younger, most all of their fishing efforts were in vain unless closely supervised, as they found that throwing rocks in the water was much more fun than being quiet and patiently waiting for a fish to take their bait.

Until our oldest children were ready to take fishing seriously, I used to let them have their fun all day, scaring the fish away with their noisy activities, then fish by myself after they went to bed or early in the morning. Then, to satisfy their craving to catch a fish of their own, I would re-hook on the end of each of their fishing poles the fish *I* caught and throw the fish back into the lake when the children weren't looking. I would invite all of the

"Mom, look what we caught!"

children back down to the water's edge, telling them I already threw their lines out to help them get started. With little kids, it was easy to pull off this trick, telling them that there was a fish on their line and watching them squeal with delight as they reeled it in. Whether the fish were dead or alive, the children's response was always the same. Generally, I made sure the fish was already dead. The children would drag the poor creature up the bank and run as fast as they could to show Mommy. It made me chuckle to see how they used to wonder how come Daddy never caught any fish and only the kids did.

A rewarding benefit of camping in the mountains is the fresh mountain air. I find that we all seem to sleep easier on our camps, and I believe it is because of the fresher, cleaner air.

A common complaint I hear from unsuccessful campers is that they never have a good night's sleep because they freeze, or the bed is uncomfortable, and the list goes on. The temperature problem can be solved by covering the mattress or ground pad with a blanket and piling any extra ones on top. Some backpacking sleeping bags are designed so well that no blankets are needed. The only dilemma we faced besides these amenities was how to keep our heads from getting cold at night. We have found a few remedies.

A knit cap or hat works well for keeping your head warm, but it can come off in the night. If you don't care for the hat idea, here's one we use the most.

When you set up the beds in your tent, make a barrier above the pillow area up toward the wall of the tent. Most of the time, the slope of the hill dictates which direction the pillows will be. Make the blanket barrier higher above your head and curve it around the pillow area. This way, your pillow sits down in a bird's nest fashion, keeping your head warm on all sides. Since heat rises, the warmth from your head will rise above your pillow as you breathe, keeping the colder air from settling down.

The next thing we do is wear hooded sweat shirts when we sleep, or we use sleeping bags that have a hooded section with cinch strings. A good night's sleep is the best part of the whole camping trip for me.

Since we are on the subject of sleeping, I would like to address another safety concern here, that of lightning. I recall many a night when we all cowered in our sleeping bags while an electrical storm rumbled through the area. These are spectacular to watch, but are also extremely dangerous. In the state where I live, lightning is the number one weather-related killer.

If you are inside your tent when lightning is striking the area, you are not necessarily safe just because you are in a tent. Occasional news reports tell of lightning bouncing off trees and killing or injuring campers in tents. If a lightning storm approaches, you would be most wise to wait out the storm inside your vehicle and enjoy the show there. If you are caught in a storm while hiking, **do not run under a tree!** This is the most vulnerable place you can be as a target. Get in a low lying area away from taller structures or under a ledge and wait it out.

If you have the good fortune of having an undisturbed night's rest, I recommend that you take an early morning walk before the sun rises. Some of the most treasured experiences I remember were taking short walks early in the morning. Early morning walks allow you to see nature's beauty come to life. It's almost a spiritual experience to sit and watch the sun peek over the glowing edge of a mountain and pour its silent but majestic light over the area.

Most of your activities will be dictated by the area you choose to camp in and what attractions there are to see. We have our favorite areas in our agenda that are designated specifically for fishing, and others where we just want to relax in the pines and watch the kids play. The more you camp, the more you will find yourself returning to favorite spots and developing traditions for the area. A favorite camping place becomes even better if you return to it year after year; it makes you feel like you're coming to visit an old friend each time you arrive.

Notes

_____
_____
_____
_____
_____
_____
_____
_____
_____
_____
_____
_____
_____
_____
_____
_____
_____
_____
_____
_____
_____
_____
_____
_____

Notes

Chapter 6

COOKING DUTCH OVEN STYLE

Some years ago, our family was camping on the shores of Flaming Gorge Reservoir, just north of the Wyoming border. We were about to throw some juicy steaks on the grill when a terrible windstorm came up.

The thought of sand mixed with our feast did not appeal to us, so we sat in the tent and played games to wait out the storm. The storm didn't end, at least not until the next day.

After playing so many games and running out of things to do, I sat peering through the tent door and watched the waves crashing against the shore and every loose twig being blown through the air like a mini-spear. We were getting hungry and were lucky enough to have brought along some canned food just in case. There I sat, carving spoonfuls of cold chili out of a can as the scene before me blew by. Yuck. I started wondering how in the world traveling settlers in the 1800s would have dealt with this dilemma. They certainly didn't have RVs, and they had to have had some way of getting hot meals even in bad weather.

Later I was introduced to the Dutch oven. It is nothing more than a cast-iron kettle-type pot with three short legs and a lid with a rim around the top perimeter. A handle or "bail" allows you to carry it around.

A little subsequent research answered my question about the early settlers. The Dutch oven was used almost exclusively by the Lewis and Clark expedition for their cooking needs across the country, and many settlers traveling across the continent used it as well.

I found that you can cook anything in a Dutch oven that you can cook in a conventional oven, or even on a stove top. I also learned that it can be used in inclement weather, providing you get a head start on cooking.

I was intrigued enough to buy one of the ovens and found they come in many different sizes and styles. We took our first one to some mountains in Colorado, along with a beginner cookbook on the subject, and cooked our first Dutch oven chicken dinner. I was so impressed with the taste, texture, and simplicity of the meal that I was hooked. I promised my wife I would fix dinner on every camp from then on if I could do it in a Dutch oven.

Since that time I have acquired a whole set of different sized Dutch ovens and have had Dutch oven parties for many people around town. I have ended up doing classes for groups, and eventually became the chairperson for our city's annual Dutch oven cookoff every Fourth of July. If you learn to cook Dutch oven style, you'll become very popular with those who eat your food!

One of the nicest things about a Dutch oven is that you can invert the lid on some rocks or pieces of brick and you have a

Dutch ovens come in a variety of sizes

very handy frying pan. In short, we found that we had to take only one Dutch oven for all our cooking needs, thus eliminating the need for several pans or a griddle.

The query I had in my mind, back on that windy day at Flaming Gorge, was answered by my Dutch ovens. Anyone can cook exotic meals of any kind in *any* weather conditions. I went to great extremes to prove this.

I cooked a mouth-watering au jus roast on my patio, the second week of January during a fierce blizzard. The temperature outside was nine degrees below zero. The roast featured potatoes and carrots in a tantalizing au jus sauce and was something to make you drool.

I fixed a chocolate mayonnaise cake with raspberry sauce in a bundt pan *inside* my Dutch oven while on a fossil expedition with the family in the remote western deserts of Utah. I had to chuckle at myself as I opened the lid to the completed masterpiece while coyotes were howling up on a nearby hill. What a contrast!

I make whole wheat rolls and breads, pies, pastries, vegetable dishes, main courses—you name it, I've done it—all on outdoor camps and also at home. The most memorable cookout was when I was asked to chef the meals for a group of Scouts on a January winter camp. The temperature was three degrees below zero, and it was very difficult to keep things from freezing.

I served those voracious boys Hawaiian pork chops, rolls, and side vegetables. The food was great, and we ate around the fire. The cold temperatures created some interesting events during dinner though, in that while I was leaning over the plate on my lap, my coat hat strings settled into the sauce on my meat. Within seconds, the strings were frozen to the sauce. When I stood up to add some wood to our fire, the boys burst into a roar of laughter. The frozen strings caused my pork chop to lift off my plate and dangle around my neck. They talked about it for weeks after.

Now for how you can be a Dutch oven chef in your circle of acquaintances, or just the family cook at camp.

Purchasing a Dutch Oven and Accessories

Dutch ovens can be purchased at a variety of sporting and hardware stores. If this is your first time buying one, you should consider what size you will want to use most and perhaps buy different sizes later. You can cook most meals for a small or medium-sized family in a 12" oven.

Dutch ovens come in sizes ranging from 8 to 22 inches in diameter. I've seen some monster sizes, and they are normally used for large groups, but that will come later in your skills.

Make sure the oven you are buying has a nice snug fit when you put the lid on. Since Dutch ovens are self-basting, an improperly fitting lid can inhibit the quality of your cooking.

I recommend that you purchase some accessory tools to go with your oven. They are—

- A lid lifter for lifting off the very hot lid.
- A lid stand—a sanitary place to set the hot lid while checking your food.
- A small whisk broom for brushing off coals from the lid.
- Long tongs for putting briquettes on the lid and underneath the oven.
- A briquette starter, which consists of a flue-style pipe with a grate about halfway down inside and an insulated handle. A wad of newspapers under the grate is all you need to ignite the briquettes on top of the grate. The concentrated heat from the papers ignites the lowest briquettes, which in turn light the others above them, thus eliminating the need for lighter fluids.
- Briquettes. They are the most preferred heat source for Dutch ovens, although wood coals can be used if necessary.

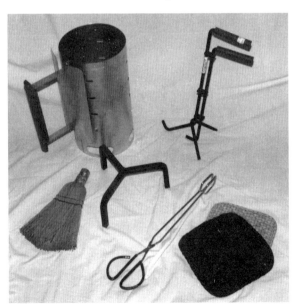

Dutch oven accessories. Clockwise from upper left: briquette lighter, lid lifter, hot pads, tongs, and whisk broom; lid stand in the middle.

Briquettes are much easier to cook with, taking up less space than wood coals and having more accuracy in cooking times.
- Hot pads or mittens are always handy in cooking.
- Long serving utensil—keep it with your oven set for easy serving.

Along with your cooking accessories, you will need two more things, which you probably have around the house:
- Cooking oil
- Paper towels

Seasoning Your Dutch Oven

A new cast-iron Dutch oven will have a wax-like coating on it from the manufacturer to protect it from rusting during distribution. When you get it home, wash it inside and out with warm soapy water and dry it thoroughly.

The seasoning process creates a permanent, long lasting coating which makes your oven stick-free. After seasoning, you should never wash the oven (with soap) again or the seasoning will come off. With use, the seasoning develops into a coating that gives Dutch oven food its unique flavor.

To start, make sure your oven is dry after you have washed it for the first time. Using a paper towel, wipe on a coat of vegetable or salad oil, inside and out, and on both sides of the lid. Place the oven inside your conventional oven, with the lid ajar. Bake your new oven at 250 degrees for about an hour and a half. Let it cool completely. Your oven is now ready for use.

For the first few meals, you will want to avoid foods that use acidic ingredients such as tomato sauces, in that they can undo a new seasoning job. Try doing chicken or bread recipes for the first two or three times, and your seasoning will be well developed for any recipe. A well-seasoned oven gradually turns dark shiny black with use.

A well-seasoned oven is easy to clean, providing you don't burn anything. Simply scrape out the food, scrub out any remaining food with just a little water and a plastic pot scrubber, then wipe it out. Wipe on a light coat of oil, and that's it. When you use your oven again, wipe on fresh oil and preheat the oven to prepare the seasoning, as well as to sterilize the inside to accommodate food. I found that wiping out the inside of my oven with a light amount of bacon grease neutralizes any stale aromas that might have lingered from oil or long-term storage.

When you store your oven between uses, always put a folded-up paper towel between the lid and oven to absorb any moisture and to allow ventilation to keep the oil coating from becoming rancid.

Heat Control

Some people excavate large holes on their camping trips to bury their Dutch ovens in, with a configuration of coals around the oven. Although this method is popular with some folks, I never found it necessary. True, the insulative factors of "underground" cooking will allow slow cooking for several hours, but cooking in simpler above-ground techniques has been just fine even for my beef briskets and turkeys.

Wood coals have been the traditional heat source since Colonial times, but modern-day briquettes are by far the most convenient way to go.

If you prefer to cook with wood coals, you will need two pits, one for the fire and one for the oven. The coals will have to be changed frequently since they soon lose their heating capacity.

The problem that most beginners stumble into with briquettes is they underestimate the heat concentration of just one briquette. You need fewer briquettes than you think.

I remember another chicken dinner we cooked on a fishing trip when it started to rain. (Seems like I had bad weather on all my trips, doesn't it? Honestly, though, bad weather has always been the exception.) I started to pile rocks around my Dutch oven to keep the raindrops off. I assumed that since the temperature was dropping and it was wet outside, I would need more briquettes. I had my dinner in a 10" oven and had only ten briquettes on the lid and nine underneath. I added about six more briquettes, top and bottom to compensate for what I thought should be done.

Usually, chicken in a 10" oven would be fully cooked in 1 1/2 to 2 hours. I let the chicken cook for 1 hour and 45 minutes and pulled off the lid, only to find that the only dinner I had for that day was a solid black brick of charred chicken meat. So go easy on the heat.

For medium cooking heats, I generally place enough briquettes on the lid and underneath so that they are spaced one briquette width apart. You can easily adjust the heat in your oven by using more or fewer briquettes depending on what you are cooking.

Here is a basic guide to get you started:

For cooking meat dishes:

10" oven—10 briquettes top, 9 on the bottom.

12" oven—14 briquettes top, 10 on the bottom.

For cooking breads and cakes:

10" oven—9 briquettes top, 5 on the bottom in a circle.

12" oven—14 briquettes top, 6 on the bottom in a circle.

You'll notice that with bread, I use almost half as many briquettes on the bottom as I do the top.

Don't fret just yet into thinking that you'll have no idea as to what and how to fix; at the end of this chapter I'll leave you with some simple recipes with complete briquette numbers.

If you're ever uncertain, you won't hurt your tasty creation by lifting the lid to check it while it cooks. Cooking with a Dutch oven does take practice, but after a meal or two, you'll be surprised at how easy it is.

Now you're probably wondering how I cook our meals in inclement weather. I have two methods: at home I use my Dutch ovens *inside* an outdoor barbecue. On camps, I surround my ovens with rocks and cover them with an inverted fire pan.

At home I found that a briquette barbecue grill was perfect for the task, especially on our patio. Gas barbecues are tough to use for this purpose, so if you know someone who is getting rid of their briquette barbecue, do them a favor—take it off their hands.

You can use a full-size barbecue or the smaller portable type. It is best to use a barbecue with a closeable lid. Some Dutch oven wizards I know cook on metal tables or on the ground out in the open. This is fine, and many champion "Dutchers" do it that way. But when briquettes are in the open, they burn out faster, especially if a breeze comes up, thus causing the briquettes to burn hotter and cause hot spots on your dinner. Also, cooking on an open metal table is prohibitive in rainy weather. If your briquettes burn out too fast, you will need to add more half way through. I also find the closeable barbecue safer to use around children at home.

Once you have your barbecue (and you may want to purchase a nice one, large enough to hold two ovens at a time), remove the food rack and place an old pizza pan or series of pieces of bricks to rest your oven on. Although some Dutch ovens have legs, my experiences have shown that the distance between the legs and the bottom of the oven is too small for the briquettes and the heat will be too intense. I normally place three small pieces of brick as a tripod support, with the edges of the oven resting on them and the briquettes in between. Since I began doing that, I have never burned anything in the bottom.

When your food is in the oven and ready and the briquettes are all lit, use your tongs to set each briquette in place on the bottom, then set your oven carefully over them. Then close the cover and place the necessary amount of briquettes on the lid. You can then let it snow, rain, or whatever. Your briquettes will do the job undisturbed.

This is a good place for a safety note. Briquettes are powerful when lit. Although they are a safe fuel source for storage, they can be a challenge to extinguish. Use common sense and **never use briquettes indoors. They give off noxious fumes that can be fatal.** Use your briquettes in a safe place in your yard, away from flammable items, like your house or other structures, and never leave them unattended. Always keep water nearby in case you drop a briquette. And since you are putting a Dutch oven in a barbecue, make sure the one you are using is structurally capable of supporting a **full** oven. Many of them are, but there are others that are so flimsy they could collapse if even too many burger patties were on them. A Dutch oven is heavy by itself, being cast iron, and is even heavier when full of food.

If you don't have a yard or patio, try using your Dutch oven *in* your conventional oven and cook without briquettes. You may not have the same control with top and bottom heat adjustments on some recipes, but you can come really close.

The second method I use, is of course, on camps. In some supermarkets in spring and summer, you've probably noticed those inexpensive table top barbecues that are nothing more than a round pan with a wire rack, and three slide-in legs which are about eight inches long. They ordinarily do not cost more than $5 to $10 on sale, but they are perfect for multiple uses outdoors. Not only can you barbecue with these on your camp, but they make an excellent lightweight fire pan for your campfires or a cover for the Dutch oven.

I place an old pizza pan on the ground or in an existing fire pit, arrange the brick pieces and briquettes on the pan, then set the oven on top. I stack rocks around my oven, and the inverted barbecue pan goes over the top. I sometimes put a small rock on the inverted pan to keep the wind from blowing it off. You have to be careful if you use a barbecue at home, or stack rocks around your oven, so that you don't cut off the oxygen supply to the briquettes, or they will slowly go out. Typically, a wall of rocks like a fire pit has enough cracks between the stones to let in just the right amount of air.

Both these methods have been used in snowstorms, pouring rain, and windstorms, and dinner was always on time.

You can conserve the amount of briquettes even further by stacking your ovens one atop the other. The briquettes on the lid of one can heat the bottom of the oven on top. The only difficulty with this method is that you have to unstack the ovens to check the food of the oven on the bottom.

Besides the benefits of Dutch ovens in camping, they are fabulous emergency items to have at home in case of a power outage or natural disaster. Briquettes are safe and easy to store, and Dutch oven cooking skills will be an asset to you in the event of such a crisis. Again, never use briquettes indoors!

Planning your meals is as essential as making a plan for the activities on your camp, as discussed in chapter two. If I feel that I am going to be wanting some rest on a camp, I plan very simple, throw-together meals, and cook only when I have to. If I am out for a good time and have a few days to get into the cooking scene, I bring all the trimmings and the whole spice rack!

Along with your daily routine schedule that you put together, list all your meals and what they will consist of. Next, make an "ingredients list" of the things you will need to buy for those meals. Here's an example:

Day 1:		Ingredients List
Breakfast:	Cereal and fruit	1. Cereal
	Juice	2. Milk

Lunch:	Deli sandwiches	3. Apples
	Yogurt	4. Juice
Dinner:	Dutch oven chicken	5. Deli rolls
	Side vegetables	6. Ham & turkey
Day 2:		7. Lettuce
Breakfast:	Bacon & eggs	8. Tomatoes
	Toast, juice	9. Yogurt
Lunch:	Light snacks	10. Chicken
	Vegetables & dip	11. BBQ sauce
Dinner:	Tacos	12. Frozen peas
	Chips & salsa	13. Bacon, eggs
Day 3:		14. Bread, butter
Breakfast:	Cereal & toast	15. Vegetables
Lunch:	Deli sandwiches	16. Sauce
(Dinner after returning home)		17. Taco shells
		18. Other & etc.

Keep your ingredients list with the packing list so that you can keep track of what needs to be packed, and keep the menu list in your cooking box to recall what you planned to eat.

Now for the recipes I promised. I have a fancy collection of recipes, and from them I'll choose the simpler ones. There are a number of gourmet Dutch oven cookbooks out there, and I encourage you to purchase one when you are ready to challenge your skills. Who knows, maybe you can start an annual cookoff where you live!

Three Favorite Main Dishes:

Honey Barbecue Chicken
Assorted chicken pieces, enough for each person
Salt & pepper

Paprika

Bottle of hickory barbecue sauce (your favorite brand will do)

Honey

Briquette guide:

10" oven—10 briquettes top, 9 bottom

12" oven—14 briquettes top, 10–12 bottom

Preheat your Dutch oven and wipe out with oil, then add a small amount of oil in the bottom. In the bottom of the oven, brown chicken pieces on all sides, sprinkling with salt, pepper, and paprika. Cover, place briquettes on the lid, and bake 30 minutes.

While chicken is baking, mix two parts barbecue sauce to one part honey in a mixing bowl; set aside.

Remove the lid, leaving briquettes in position. Carefully remove any excess oil or chicken fat. Spoon on the honey barbecue mixture over each piece, place the lid back on the oven, and bake an additional 25 minutes. Repeat basting procedure with remaining sauce and cover for 5 minutes longer, and serve.

Remember, your exact cooking times may vary depending on the depth of your oven and how much chicken you are cooking. The amount of honey barbecue sauce you prepare also depends on the amount of chicken you are fixing—about 1 to 1 1/2 cups per chicken should be enough.

Pork Chops

Pork chops, 1 to 2 per serving

Potatoes, sliced or quartered (1/2 to 1 potato per person)

1 medium onion for every 4 pork chops

Cream of mushroom soup mixed with half the amount of water called for on the can. (1 can of soup for every 5–6 chops.)

Preheat and oil your Dutch oven. Brown chops on both sides. Place chops in bottom of oven, followed by potato slices, then onions. Pour the soup mixture over all of the contents.

This works best in a 10" oven, and I recommend putting 10 briquettes on the lid and 9 on the bottom, for 55 minutes, or until potatoes are tender. The thickness of your pork chops may cause the exact cooking time to vary, so check them from time to time.

Enchiladas
1 pkg. corn or flour tortillas, usually 8–10 per pkg.
1 lb. cooked chicken pieces (we also use canned meat)
1 cup sour cream
1 can cream of mushroom soup
1 can cream of chicken soup
1 four oz. can diced green chilies
1/2 lb. grated cheese

In a mixing bowl, combine chicken pieces, sour cream, soups, and chilies. Spoon this mixture onto the tortillas and roll up, saving about 1/2 cup of the mixture for later use. Place the rolled tortillas in the bottom of a 12" Dutch oven. Pour the remaining filling mixture over the filled tortillas, then sprinkle the grated cheese on top.

Bake with 16 briquettes on top and 7 on the bottom in a circle for 1 hour. Serves 6.

Three Favorite Side Dishes:

Corn Cobbettes with Potatoes
This recipe is easy to put together and can serve a lot of people.
12" Dutch oven
Potatoes, 1–2 per person, sliced
1 square of margarine or butter
1 onion for every 4 potatoes
Corn cobs, cut in halves or thirds
Salt & Pepper

Preheat and oil your Dutch oven. Melt a small amount of margarine in the bottom. Place half of the sliced potatoes in the bottom of the oven. Sprinkle on salt and pepper. Add a few onion slices. Then add all of the corn cobs, drizzled with margarine or butter. Add remaining potatoes and onions on top. Sprinkle with salt and pepper, and a few remaining dabs of butter. Cover, and bake with 14 briquettes on top and 12 on the bottom for 40–50 minutes. Remove lid, and drizzle a small amount of margarine or butter over it just before serving.

Garden Vegetable Supreme

4 med. size yellow crookneck squash, sliced
1 small green pepper, chopped
1 small red pepper, chopped
7 green onions, chopped
1 cup your favorite salsa
1 cup grated mozzarella cheese
1 tablespoon margarine

Melt margarine in bottom of 10" oven. Layer squash, peppers and onions in bottom. Pour salsa over all and sprinkle with the cheese. Bake with 10 briquettes on top and 7 on the bottom for 30–45 minutes.

Ken's Rolls

10" version:
1/3 cup powdered milk (in powder form)
1 cup warm water
1/4 cup sugar
1 tablespoon yeast
1 egg
3 tablespoons melted butter or margarine
1/2 teaspoon salt

1 1/2 cup freshly ground whole wheat flour

1 1/2 cup white flour

In a mixing bowl combine milk powder and sugar with warm water. Sprinkle on yeast and stir in. Wait 5 minutes. Add egg, butter, and salt. Stir. Add wheat flour, stir until smooth. Add remaining flour, 1/2 cup at a time, until a workable dough forms. Cover, let rise 45 minutes in a warm area. Oil and warm a 10" oven. Remove dough from bowl, knead until smooth, cut into 8 equal sections, knead each one into a ball and place in oven. Cover, and let rise 30 minutes while briquettes are lighting.

After 30 minutes or when the briquettes are ready (whichever comes first), place 9 briquettes on the lid and 5 on the bottom for 25 minutes. Baste tops of rolls with butter when done. 12" oven guide: 1 1/2 times this recipe, 14 briquettes on the top, and 6 on the bottom for 25–30 minutes. Makes 12.

Three Favorite Desserts:

Your Basic Cobbler

Whenever I talk to someone who has had a little exposure to Dutch ovens, the most common dish they make reference to is a cobbler. These have been popular for years, and surprisingly enough for me, some people I have met think that the *only* things you cook in a Dutch oven are cobblers.

The basic cobbler consists of prepared fruit, poured into the bottom of a Dutch oven, and a cake mix batter dumped on top of it. That's all there is to it.

You can choose any fruit you like, from canned or bottled peaches, to cherries. Usually 2–3 cans are adequate for a 12" oven. When you prepare the cake mix, most people substitute 1/4 cup water for the egg, so that the batter doesn't rise and burn on the underside of the lid.

Cobblers take anywhere from 30 minutes to an hour to cook. The most useful method to check it is to poke a toothpick into the center of the cake. If the toothpick comes out clean, you're ready to enjoy the cobbler.

Serve some whipped cream or ice cream along with your cobbler to really enhance the treat.

Experiment with different fruits and amounts, and see which you like best. Here's one of mine:

Blackberry/Blueberry Cobbler Pie
This is not your "traditional" cobbler, but whenever I make it, there are never any leftovers!

2 cups fresh, frozen, or canned blackberries
1 cup fresh, frozen, or canned blueberries
1 cup white flour
1 cup whole wheat flour
2 teaspoons baking powder
1/4 teaspoon salt
1/2 cup margarine, softened
1 cup sugar
3/4 cup milk
2/3 cup sugar
Powdered sugar
Ice cream or whipped cream (optional)

Thaw fruit, if frozen. In a medium mixing bowl, mix together flours, baking powder, and salt. Beat margarine and the 1 cup sugar until fluffy. Add flour mixture alternately with milk. Beat until smooth. Spread batter evenly over the bottom of a greased 10" oven. Flare up the edges of the batter similar to a pie.

Sprinkle bottom crust with all the fruit. Sprinkle 2/3 cup sugar over it, depending on the sweetness of the fruit. Bake 45 minutes with 10 briquettes on the top and 6 on the bottom. Sprinkle lightly with powdered sugar. Serve with ice cream or whipped cream. Serves 12.

Pineapple Upside-Down Cake
This one is a real eye catcher as well as a delicious treat.
1/2 cup brown sugar
1/4 cup butter
Maraschino cherries
1 can sliced pineapple
1 yellow cake mix

Put butter and brown sugar in a 14" oven and melt while stirring over a warm fire or briquettes (a 12" oven can be used, although a 14" oven provides more surface area). Place the pineapple slices close together in the butter and sugar mixture, and place the halved maraschino cherries in each pineapple center. In a separate container prepare the cake mix according to the instructions on the package. Pour batter over pineapple and place lid on Dutch oven. Place oven over 7 briquettes, with 17 on the lid, for 40 minutes, or until golden brown. Cool 10 minutes. While this is cooling, cut a piece of cardboard into a circle the same diameter as the cake in the oven, or if you're lucky enough to have a pizza pan the same size, use that. Cover the cardboard with aluminum foil, and place on the cake. Turn the oven upside down to remove the cake. This is also a good chance to see how well seasoned your oven is by how much the cake sticks. If your oven is well seasoned, the cake should just fall right out and a beautiful mouthwatering creation will present itself before your guests. A little cream and you've got it made.

Breakfast Idea (When the wind isn't blowing)
One of my favorite things to do on a camp is to rise and shine with bacon, eggs, and toast from my Dutch oven. I simply place the

Dinner is served! Clockwise from top left: Honey Barbecue Chicken, Ken's Rolls, Pineapple Upside-down Cake, and Garden Vegetable Supreme.

lid upside down on some rocks or small pieces of brick and the oven next to it. The eggs are fried in the oven, while the bacon is done on the lid. When the bacon is done, I wipe off the lid with a paper towel, butter some slices of bread, and grill them to a toasty brown. My kids love it . . . my daughter calls it "Campin' Toast."

Notes

Notes

Chapter 7

FIRST AID AND EMERGENCIES

You probably can't count the times you've been on an outing somewhere and cut your finger or got a sliver in your hand with no way to remove it. Or, have you ever been the first at the scene of a serious automobile accident and wished you had some way to help?

As often as we have been camping, first-aid supplies have sure come in handy.

You should have two kits in your vehicle at all times—a first-aid kit and supplies, and an emergency survival kit. The first-aid kit deals with injuries, and the emergency survival kit handles being stranded.

Prevention is heralded as the best medicine, and you should always use precaution in all your activities. There will be times when an accident causes injuries that you are prepared to handle. Then again, some injuries are too severe for a first-aid kit alone to adequately deal with.

Once we camped on the top of one of the most beautiful mountain ranges in our area. We spent a wonderful day with the family, and my wife was fixing dinner while I went for a little walk with our daughter Angela, age two at the time.

I was some distance from camp when I heard my wife call that dinner was ready. With my little sweetheart holding my pinky finger with her entire hand, we walked slowly back to camp. I was musing and appreciating one of those precious moments of fatherhood, watching my daughter toddle along chattering happily.

As we were walking, Angela stumbled on a small sticker bush and started to fall. The almost instinctive reaction was in force, my hand quickly wrapped around hers, and I gently lifted her over the bush, preventing her fall. At the instant I lifted her up, she let out a scream of unmistakable pain.

What have I done? I thought as I held her up. She was crying horribly, like small children do when they are in very intense pain. Hurriedly, I ran back to camp while Angela continued to scream incessantly.

Carefully, I laid our little one on a bed. With her mother near her, she calmed down a bit, but whenever we touched her hand or arm, she screamed. I was sick. I thought I must have broken her little arm when I picked her up.

We quickly extinguished our fire and left our dinner. All of us piled in the van, and off we went. It took nearly an hour for us to get off the mountain, every bump adding to our daughter's discomfort, and my frantic driving probably didn't help. I'd have done anything to stop her pain, and I felt horrible.

We drove to the nearest town that was large enough to have a hospital.

In the emergency room, the attending doctor examined our girl. Watching her suffer for something I somehow did was all I could stand.

The doctor held up a candy sucker in front of Angela and restrained her good arm to see if she could move the injured one at all. She just cried harder. After a few touches with his hand up and down her arm, he turned to me and said, "I get quite a few of you daddies in here with injuries to their kids like this. Usually this problem is from twirling and swinging their kids. Your daughter's elbow is dislocated."

The doctor told my wife to hold onto Angela tightly, because his solution would be momentarily painful. Quickly, he grabbed Angela's arm, and she screamed like a siren. The doctor seemed to wrench her arm back and forth until we all heard a faint "pop." At that very instant, and still crying, Angela reached up with the *injured* arm and grabbed the sucker out of the doctor's pocket and screamed, "Mine!" Then the crying stopped.

"Will she need some painkiller?" I asked.

"No, she'll be painless and fine in two minutes," the doctor chuckled.

He was right. Within minutes, Angela was running up and down the hall in the hospital as though it never happened—sucker in mouth and all. I was bewildered, but still shaken from the event, and even more so when I got the $160 bill. To this day I have never again swung my daughter or lifted any of our kids by one arm.

This incident illustrates how a peaceful camp can be turned into an emergency within seconds. Emergencies happen when you least expect one. This is why you should be prepared as much as possible for the "unforeseen."

Prevention goes beyond having medical supplies on hand. It involves safety practices and eliminating such risky outdoor activities as swimming without a life jacket or climbing dangerous cliffs. Common sense will make most considerations of this subject obvious. In this book I can't deal with every safety issue, so use caution to avoid accidents. Sometimes encounters with wild animals can pose dangers, and I urge all campers to find out what precautions you should take to avoid any hazards related to terrain or wildlife in the area you will be camping—before you leave.

Your first-aid kit should be in your vehicle whether you are camping or not. It should contain an updated supply of first-aid materials that you check each time you go camping. You can purchase an already packaged kit, or you can put together one of your own.

If you put together your own, a plastic box is ideal. Here are some suggested items to have in it.

First-Aid Kit

First-aid manual
Laxatives
Diarrhea medicine
Soap
Gauze
Triangular bandage (sling)
Cotton balls
Safety pins
Thermometer
Disposable diapers (for dressing major wounds)
Tweezers
Matches
Alcohol prep pads
Individual medicines
CPR rescue breather
First-aid spray

Aspirin or pain relievers
Rubbing alcohol
Petroleum jelly
Salt
Bandages, assorted sizes
Elastic bandage
Cotton swabs
Scissors
Sanitary napkins (pressure dressing)
Tape
Needles
Small splints (popsicle sticks)
String
Antibacterial ointment
Latex gloves
Instant cold pack

It's a very good idea to take a first-aid class with your spouse or a friend, if you do not have some first-aid training. The classes in the community are very inexpensive—sometimes free of charge. The first aid you learn may save the life of someone you love.

The other kit you should always keep in your vehicle may come in handy if you are ever stranded on a highway somewhere, especially in winter.

When I was a Boy Scout, we made car survival kits out of the material from an old pair of jeans and filled them with articles from around the house. I still have one and keep it in my van.

Here's what's in it:

Car Survival Kit

Pocket mirror	Compass
Large candle	Waterproof tape
Tin can	Electrical tape
Space blanket	Small garden shovel
Siphon tubing	Quarters
Sewing kit	Pocket knife
Bouillon cubes	Matches (waterproof)
Water purification tablets	Heat packs
Lighter fluid	Cigarette lighter
String	Separate food pack

The separate food pack is actually a rotatable 72-hour food kit that fits into an empty half-gallon milk container. It contains:

Day 1:
Breakfast:
    1 granola bar
    Hot chocolate

Lunch:
   1 beef jerky stick
   Apple cider
Dinner:
   1 pkg. soup
   3 crackers
Snacks:
   4 pieces hard candy

Day 2:
Breakfast:
   Hot chocolate
   1/2 Package trail mix
Lunch:
   Beef jerky stick
   Fruit snacks
   Apple cider
Dinner:
   Soup
   3 crackers
Snacks:
   4 pieces candy
   Gum

Day 3:
Breakfast:
   Apple juice (in can)
   1/2 package trail mix
Lunch:
   Soup
Dinner:
   Granola bar
   Fruit snack

Snack:
    3 pieces of candy
    2 sticks gum
Water Source: Empty 2-liter plastic pop bottle cleaned and
    filled with clean water.

The contents of the food pack are certainly not filet mignon, but they will keep you alive for several days. If you make your own kits, you may want to tailor the kit to suit your family's needs (or appetite!).

I can't say that I have ever been stranded somewhere to the point I had to rely entirely on my kits, although I have been known to pilfer the candy out of them from time to time while on business trips.

Notes

Chapter 8

THE ENVIRONMENT IS YOURS!

The more time passes, the more I hear the word *environment* in literature, the media, and in casual conversation. It has become something that is vital for all of us to be concerned about.

Back in the homesteading days, there was less to throw away, and less to worry about if you did throw something away. Mother Nature had her own slow steady pace of healing what was done. The problem today is that Mother Nature can't keep up with the rate that things are being destroyed or disposed of. Worse yet, with modern-day technology, an increasing amount of disposable packaging adds to the amount of trash being discarded in the outdoors.

Since there are more people frequenting wilderness areas, efforts have been beefed up to keep these areas as pristine as when they were found. Unfortunately, public land officials cannot conserve these areas without the public's help.

We've all seen the effects of careless use or malicious vandalism on nature. Some forest areas are closed because they were literally ruined by the actions of just a few individuals who lacked the integrity to do otherwise.

Also, there are areas closed to the use of camping—not necessarily from vandalism but simply from normal use.

Many people unknowingly harm the natural balance of the area which they are in because they simply do not know what they need to be doing to counteract the effects of their use on the land.

I've collected several travel brochures from the state in which I live. Among them are the publications from the National Forest Service and the Bureau of Land Management. The central theme that is coming of age from these agencies is "Leave No Trace." In brief, this theme applies to everything you do in the outdoors and should be the consideration you give to any activity before you start it.

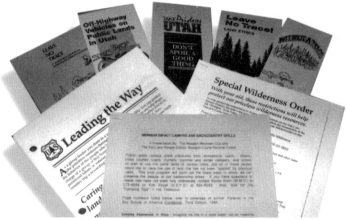

There are countless publications available to the public regarding care of the environment.

The general effort I observe from the publications from these government agencies is to create an awareness of what the problems are and to *educate* the public about how they can help. Anyone who ventures into the outdoors has the responsibility of doing his or her part to properly care for the environment. We should learn to do what we can to minimize the impact of our use on public lands.

It has been said that we used to talk about people surviving in the wilderness, but now we talk about the wilderness surviving us. We need to educate ourselves and others about what we can do as individuals to maintain the beauty of our national forests and public lands. The best thing is education. Education creates conscience, and conscience begets more responsible behavior. If we practice sound principles, then our children will follow our example and do likewise.

There are several things campers unknowingly do that deteriorate a beautiful camp area. Along with each of these areas of concern, I will discuss methods that can prevent the problems.

A few individuals complain that if they follow all the conservation techniques every agency wants done, camping is more work than it's worth. This was true in some cases, but we found ways to adapt to environmentally protective practices and make our camping routine easier at the same time.

Let's talk about the most common concerns addressed by forest and national park publications.

The most prevalent of concerns over the years is litter. Much campaigning has been done to encourage people not to litter. The saddest part about litter in any outdoor setting is that there is no excuse for it at all. Anyone who has the means to pack rubbish into the wilderness also has the means to pack it out.

Along with every pack list should be plenty of trash bags to pack out items of disposal. We always keep a trash bag handy in

Forest signs often carry reminders of our responsibilities.

our tent or hung up in our camp area to simplify disposal of any paper or empty containers.

One important tip should be mentioned here. Never leave trash bags open on the ground, as nocturnal animals will some-times sniff them out at night and make a mess with the contents. In some areas, the smell can attract bears that are scavenging for food.

Plastic handled grocery bags are very convenient to use for trash. Simply wrap a bungee cord around a tree and the bag can hang from one of the bungee hooks. Never nail anything to trees.

One additional tip you may want to incorporate into your family camping, which we've done with our children, is to make the campsite a better place than when you found it. Most of the time it simply involves picking up any trash leftover from previous campers and it takes only a few minutes.

The next item of concern is what to do when "nature calls." With RVs it's not a problem, but with backpacking and tent/car camping, it must be dealt with carefully.

Occasionally when camping as a family, we found clumps of soiled toilet paper behind nearby trees along with uncovered human waste. Not only is this repulsive, but it creates an annoyance in that flies are attracted from everywhere.

In many forest and outdoor publications, campers are urged to locate latrines at least 200 feet from any waterway or campsite. When backpacking, a latrine or "cat hole" is one feasible way to properly dispose of human waste. Tent camping from your vehicle allows for other options. If a latrine is used by a group of people, the latrine should be dug 6 to 12 inches deep and each use should be covered over with a small amount of soil to deter flies. When you break camp, the latrine should be completely covered, with twigs and leaves scattered for camouflage.

If you are camping with family, and possibly other friends, many drawbacks to the latrine can come into play. First, privacy is at risk, especially if two people arrive at the same time. Second, hiking 200 feet to the latrine at 2:00 AM is an eerie thing for a lot of us—likewise perching in a precarious position at that time of the morning. Stories of Big Foot stalking the woods at night always seem to cross my mind when I'm in those circumstances. Third, I would feel even better if I didn't have to even dig a hole and have the "toilet" closer to camp, thus eliminating trails in vegetation as well.

After trying a number of different things over the past decade, we've found that a portable toilet has the most benefit. Some "die-hards" might turn their noses up at the idea, but the ladies at my campsite are grateful for the convenience. And if you have children in the potty-training stage, it's nice to not have to go for a hike several times an hour—and at the worst times.

Along with our portable toilet, we found some tent-bathroom stalls which offer the necessary privacy so that the "outhouse" can be a little closer to camp. With this method, privacy is not a problem, it's more comfortable, less awkward, and the journey at night is safer. It also appeals to the utmost of the "Leave No Trace" ethics.

There are two more benefits we found with this arrangement. If you throw a rubber mat in the tent stall and close the lid on the toilet, you can sit with a pot of warm water and enjoy a refreshing sponge bath during extended camping trips.

The second benefit is at home. Have you ever had the inconvenience of the water lines being shut off in your neighborhood due to construction or possibly a disaster of some kind? What would you do if you could not use your toilet? A portable toilet in your home storage is a handy replacement in case of emergencies.

Most portable toilets require that you add a tank deodorizer chemical to deal with the waste. They ordinarily have their own water reservoir, to operate the flushing mechanism. After your camp, you simply empty the toilet tank (some detach separately) into a dump station or a regular toilet. All of the portable toilets I've seen are small and compact for easy storage or packing— perfect for the family camper.

If the portable toilet does not appeal to you, nor does taking precautions in latrine use, then you may want to consider camping in established campgrounds with sanitary facilities already in place.

Next among our concerns is the campfire. Not long ago, we arrived at a new campsite and found five separate campfire rings, all within 20 feet of each other. As I studied each of the fire pits wondering why people would go to all the trouble to gather boulders for a new ring, I soon observed why.

Each ring had become the garbage dump for the previous camper, and the next camper did not want to be responsible for digging out the old pit and going to the effort of finding a way to deal with the large pile of accumulated garbage.

There are two things you can consider when you arrive at the campsite:

First, if there already is a campfire ring, don't build another one. Use the existing one, even if you have to clean it out.

Second, if there isn't a fire pit or fire ring when you arrive, and you have no choice but to make one, dig out the soil for the fire pit in an area not too close to trees or areas with a lot of dry tinder on the ground, and save the soil to bury the campfire later. Some publications advise leaving the fire ring for others to use, or even taking the cooled ashes home for disposal.

Never leave a firemark like this.

Other publications advise not using rocks to surround the fire because of the risk of certain types of rock exploding if they become too hot.

I found yet another way to have the best of both worlds. We take a fire pan. I have used two types of fire pans, either a small table-top barbecue that you can get at the store for $5 to $10, or a cut-off portion of a metal barrel bottom propped up on a couple of rocks.

And we go a step further. Firewood in some areas is scarce, in that it is sometimes hard to come by unless you damage a few trees by tearing off the lower dry branches (something the forest service is also opposed to); so we take our own. Many cabinet mills will gladly give you their throwaway wood scraps—the best firewood I've found. I simply stop by a local mill a day or two before our camp, take in a cardboard box, and in less than a minute I have cut and dried oak and maple hardwood to burn for the entire camp. We pack the wood *in* the fire pan when we take it along. When we're breaking camp, we pour the **cold** and **water-soaked** ashes, which always amount to very little, into a bag and *voila*, no campfire marks, no mess, and it's a lot less work than slaving away with the ol' ax. No trace remains.

Sometimes forest areas have campfire and firewood restrictions. Never chop down trees or vegetation for your fire. Several areas where this violation has been prevalent have a barren look to them, in that the lower branches of trees are broken or sawed off and the area looks like a bald spot in the lush surrounding vegetation. Do all that you can to leave the surrounding vegetation as untouched as possible.

Quite a number of our camps have been without a campfire altogether. If you take a lightweight fuel stove along, or cook with a Dutch oven and fire pan, there really is no need for a campfire for cooking. I know that the campfire is a tradition for sitting around at night, but we often find it fascinating to dim the lights and look at the vast multitude of stars that are visible high in the mountains. With our camping, a campfire is mostly a luxury, not a necessity. You must be the judge of what works best for you, but always bear in mind the responsibility *you* have for the safety and cleanliness of your fire.

Another item of concern to every camper is waste water, sometimes called "grey water." This is the water you use when washing your hands or dishes, and throw away. The last thing you want to do is wash anything in rivers or waterways. These are not sinks. Instead, try using what we found to be more convenient and better for the environment.

We take along the square five-gallon white plastic jugs with a spout on them, and a plastic tub or sink that we use to pack dishes. We prop the jug on a small table with the plastic sink below it. Now you know why some people say we often do bring everything along—*including* the kitchen sink! As the plastic sink fills with used water, we do one of three things.

1. Dump the water out at a nearby dump station.
2. Pour the water in a separate closeable container for later discharge.
3. One forest ranger gave me this idea. First make sure the water is free from food particles and has as little soap in it as possible. Carry the sink to a grassy area, far from any waterways, and do a 180-degree spin, spraying the water over a large area.

The most popular habit is to dig a hole and pour the grey water in it. The problem with this method is that once the hole is covered over, animals come and sometimes dig it up because they can smell food particles or other items of interest. Another drawback is that soaps do pollute, and putting all of this in a hole concentrates the effect to one area. So why go to the trouble of digging another hole? Spare the ground vegetation and lessen the effect.

An item of noted concern among forest officials is the all-popular method of digging a trench around tents in case of rain. Usually, choosing a proper tent location can eliminate the need for the practice.

Setting up your tent on ridges, hills or near canyon walls will prevent most problems associated with drainage. Having family camped over 10 years and in numerous storms, I can count on one hand the number of times I've really needed to furrow out any run-off water, and then it only amounted to doing it on one side.

"Trenching" around tents is sometimes left by campers who are too lazy to fill them back in before they leave. Not only is this unsightly, but it can cause erosion problems later.

Try to avoid trampling down vegetation or creating trails where there aren't any. Use only existing trails and roadways.

Finally, a note about pets. An increasing number of forest areas now prohibit pets from being brought along, namely dogs, for the damage they do in leaving waste and destroying vegetation. Dogs' barking can have a negative impact on wildlife and often is a great nuisance to other campers, so if you suspect your pet may pose a problem, you may want to leave Fido home.

Noise pollution can also leave invisible marks on nature, so never take fireworks along, which are a serious fire hazard, or

Fireworks are taboo!

stereos for blasting loud music throughout the area. No one wants to listen to *your* music, so if you must have it, take headphones.

There are possibly many more things you can do to protect the environment, and if they are not mentioned here, follow the best test and ask yourself whether the thing you plan to do will leave a mark on nature or will pollute in any way. Common sense and courtesy will usually provide the answer.

Notes

_____

_____

_____

_____

_____

_____

_____

_____

_____

_____

_____

_____

_____

_____

_____

_____

_____

_____

_____

_____

_____

_____

_____

_____

_____

_____

_____

Chapter 9

TAKING DOWN CAMP

The last thing you can do to ensure that your camping trip is stress free to the end is to allow sufficient time to pack up before going home.

I have noticed from personal experience and observation of others that campers often wait until the last minute to pack before racing out of the area to get home. I suppose this results from people trying to use every minute to the fullest before they leave.

I believe this rushed approach of throwing everything in the car and hauling out creates an aftertaste that makes the whole trip feel rushed. Worse yet, this is where the care and clean up of the campsite falls short of being done properly. Clean up is also harder to do.

The pack-up can be a great deal easier if you begin packing things after they are used for the last time—a pack-as-you-go

approach. Flashlights, for example, can be put away on the morning of your last day, or sleeping bags can be rolled up as you arise.

We try to have meals on our last day that will not require
cooking, such as cold cereal, or deli sandwiches, so we can pack
up some of the cooking items after dinner the night before. This
approach spreads out the clean-up–pack-up job to minimize the
amount of time needed for the final loading. Many of these tasks
can be completed at the same time you are doing things you
would normally be doing around camp, and they can make the
domestic duties less tiresome.

As you near the departure time, take a minute to scout
through the area for any debris or paper on the ground. Even if
your family didn't leave the garbage, go the extra mile and help out.

Camp clean up can even turn into a game for children. Give
each child a trash bag and promise an award for the largest bag of

The author taking his sweet time breaking camp

trash collected. Naturally, you would award each child with a treat, say for the largest amount, or the largest number of colors of garbage, or the one with the most of one color, etc. Use your imagination to create incentives for children to help in the effort. Scouting around the camp also helps you to avoid leaving anything behind, like someone's shoe or a toy.

If you used a latrine, as mentioned in chapter 8, be sure to cover it completely, tamp it down with a shovel, and camouflage the place with ground debris, leaves, and twigs.

If you made a fire pit, scatter any rocks used and remove trash before you bury the fire pit. Although some trash, like bottles or cans, does not burn, people persist in tossing it into the fire anyway as though the fire were a garbage dump. Again, smooth over the pit with the soil you removed and camouflage the site.

A good rule of thumb is to treat the campsite as though you will be the next to use it in a few days. Who knows, if you love the area enough, you just *might* be the next one who comes back.

I recall a particular place that I fell in love with. When we went, we used our tent and a camper van. I dug wheel ruts into the ground to level the van for our bed. When we left, I forgot to fill the wheel ruts back in.

Two weeks later, we decided to return for some more great fishing at that same campsite. As we drove in, I saw wheel ruts and realized that they were the ones *I* left. At first, I thought it was very convenient to just drive up and "plop" into a level position; then I wondered how I would feel if those wheel ruts were dug by someone else. If everyone dug potholes and left them, the camp area would look like the surface of the moon. I never left wheel ruts again.

As you leave, look back on the campsite. Does it look as appealing to you as when you first arrived? Does it look better? If the answer is yes to both these questions, then you can feel good about your use of the area. After all, *your* tax dollars pay for the upkeep of these places, so it behooves all of us to take care of them.

On the way back, you can reduce the "dread" of going home, (if you had a splendid time!) by making the trip back part of the vacation. Visit another one of those historic sights or see a ghost town. Whenever possible, I avoid taking a major interstate route home; rather I take the smaller side roads. These side roads sometimes pass through small towns where we can stop at the local park for a snack. The children always love to play on the swings, and it breaks up the journey, keeping that serene outdoor feeling with you longer.

Notes

Notes

Chapter 10

AFTER YOU'RE BACK

When you arrive home and begin to unpack, it is a good idea to leave your tent in a safe place to air out and dry. Even if it hasn't rained, moisture condensation that forms on the bottom of your tent can have disastrous results if rolled up inside. Moisture can cause mildew and mold, which literally eat the fabric.

I have close relatives who learned that lesson the hard way. They spent a night in the mountains and rolled their tent up the next morning, not remembering that the morning dew had settled on the roof of the tent.

When they went camping again a few months later, they were shocked to find that the tent roof had disintegrated from rotting mold while in storage. Had they allowed their tent to air out before storage, or at least checked it before they left, they would not have been in the predicament they were in.

As an added measure, you may want to air out sleeping bags in case of unseen dampness that can result from the tent floor. Anything that would have a risk of being damaged from mildew or mold should be aired out to dry.

After your gear is put away, make a camp journal from a lined notebook of where you went and date it. For future reference, make a lined drawing showing where the campsite is located and the conditions you encountered .

In our family travel log, we rate each camp area we've been to on a scale from one to ten, with one being poor and ten being an excellent place we would want to come back to. We list one camp per page and write what kind of fish we caught at certain places, how big they were, the best time of the year to go, certain things we would want to bring to that area, and so forth.

It may surprise you how certain items about a camp area can be forgotten though the years, but with your camp journal, you have an instant reference to recall to mind those things that you did or did not like about a particular area.

Next, I would recommend that you obtain a map of the entire area or state in which you live and mark off sections for different regions. Then arrange as many file folders as there are sections, and keep your travel brochures or local forest maps in each file about each area. This way, when you plan to visit a particular area, you can check in your file to see what activities or attractions there are for you to take advantage of, either on the way, during, or on the way back from your camp.

You can write to the county seat in each region for informational brochures about attractions, activities, or places to visit and then keep them in your files.

Depending on how intensive your records are, you can even color the roads in with a marker to show where you have been. I've done this with a map of my state for more than a decade and now it looks like a massive spider web of all the remote areas we've explored as a family. This helps us to keep track of where we haven't been yet.

Last of all, take a piece of paper and write down all the things you thought could have been better on your trip, along with some possible solutions. Survey family members and ask them the same question. This procedure led to all of the improvements we made on our camps. You can also do this while you are driving home. With these suggestions written down, keep them with your packing list so that you will be sure to make the necessary changes on the next trip.

Keep in mind that simplicity is the secret to having a great time in the outdoors. For me, being in the outdoors is the perfect antedote when I am stressed by the furious pace of daily work routines. The slower, simple lifestyle that camping provides is soothing to the nerves and makes tension subside.

Aaah!

At the moment of writing these lines, I sit near a mountain crest, marveling at a colorful scene before me. Majestic mountains, carpeted with coarse velvet pine trees, stretch for miles. The array of wildflowers, colored in vivid shades of scarlet, yellow, and lavender, are exquisite to behold. For weeks my vision has been cramped by seeing no farther than the confining walls of my home or other buildings or the distance of the car in front of me on a congested freeway. Now I am free to ponder the reaches of the horizon. What a feeling!

Take the time to observe and pay close attention to your surroundings when you go camping. The sound of a breeze gently blowing through the trees, the leaves fluttering with the breeze; the bubbling of the creek nearby, birds musically chattering, rustling noises of a squirrel in a tree, or the crisp, cool and refreshing air are all things that we sometimes forget to appreciate in our hectic society.

I've found that the slower pace lifestyle while I am surrounded by natural elements helps me to keep life in a better perspective. Perhaps it will be the same for you.

I am certain that if you go camping often with your children, you will acquire volumes of memorable stories you can recount as a family, or a library of photo albums of all the places you've been.

Of all the things that are important during our lifetimes, spending time with our families is the most significant. In retrospect, children will value the time you spend with them more than any monetary possession you give. Camping with your family takes you away from the usual daily distractions and allows you to focus mostly on your relationships. Many parents find that camping also helps troubled youth. Family camping can and will strengthen family relationships, as long as you do it properly and comfortably.

Take this book along with you on those first trips and jot down notes or items you wish to add to this information to customize your camping style. In time, you will also find that camping is *your* family's preferred outing.

HAVE FUN!

Notes

INDEX